WITHDRAWN FROM
TSC LIBRARY

WALT
WHITMAN

WALT WHITMAN

a study by

JOHN ADDINGTON SYMONDS

Benjamin Blom / Publisher

First Published 1893
Reissued 1967 by
Benjamin Blom, Inc., New York 10452
Library of Congress Catalog Card No. 67-299559

Manufactured in the United States of America

PREFACE

THIS study hardly needs an introduction. All that is wanted for a knowledge of Walt Whitman and his works is the "Complete Poems and Prose" (1888), and "Walt Whitman," by Richard Maurice Bucke, M.D. (D. Mackay, Philadelphia, 1883). I am indebted to the kindness of Mr. J. W. Wallace, of Anderton, Lancashire, for the use of copious notes from conversations with the poet, and to Dr. J. Johnston, of Bolton, for the permission to reproduce photographs taken by himself in 1890.

DAVOS PLATZ,
    March 10, 1893.

TABLE OF CONTENTS

NOTICE OF WALT WHITMAN'S LIFE

BORN in 1819 on Long Island—His ancestry—Life in boyhood at Brooklyn—Teaching school and journalism—Learns the printing trade—Youth and early manhood in New York—Descriptions of his personal appearance and qualities—Roamings through the Southern and Western States—Speculates in building—Forms the first conception of "Leaves of Grass"—Experiments in style—First edition of 1855—Its reception—Emerson, Thoreau, Lincoln—Walt adheres to his original plan—The Secession War—Hospital work—Severe illness in 1864—Paralysis in 1873—"Drum Taps" and "Democratic Vistas"—Whitman and Secretary Harlan—Whitman in the Attorney-General's office—His chronic bad health, owing to the stress of hospital-work, lays him up—Poverty—"Specimen Days"—Their value for the understanding of his character—Protracted invalidism at Camden, N.J.—Growth of his fame as writer—Devoted friends—Death in 1892 xi

STUDY OF WALT WHITMAN

I

DIFFICULTY of dealing with Whitman's work by any purely critical method—Controversies aroused by "Leaves of Grass"—The man and his personality—Leadership of a cause—Originality and largeness of scale—Impossibility of reducing his doctrine to a system—The main points of his creed 1

II

Religion—God immanent in the universe—All faith and dogmas are provisional, relative in value—Analysis of the poem "Chanting the Square Deific"—Unrestricted faith and imperturbable optimism—In what way was Whitman a Christian?—His religion corresponds to the principles of modern science—The Cosmic Enthusiasm—Its importance for the individual 13

III

Personality or Self—The meaning of egotism for Whitman—Intimate connection between man and nature—Paramount importance of a sound and self-reliant personality—All things exist for the individual—Body and soul—The ideal of athletic selfhood 36

IV

ex-Love—Amativeness and Adhesiveness—Love of women, love of comrades—Whitman's treatment of the normal sexual emotions—His relation to science—The poet's touch on scientific truths—Breadth of view—Primitive conception of sexuality and marriage—Misconceptions to which his doctrines have been exposed 54

V

The Love of comrades—"Calamus"—The ideal of a friendship, fervid, passionate, pure — Novelty of this conception—Liability to misconstruction—Question whether a new type of chivalry be not involved in the doctrine of "Calamus"—Political importance of comradeship—Speculations on the ground-stuff of "Calamus" 67

TABLE OF CONTENTS

VI

Democracy—The word *En-Masse*—Equality of human beings—Miracles are all around us in the common world—Whereever and whoever—Heroism in daily life no less than in ancient fable or religious myth—Democracy under the aspect of a new creed—Questions regarding Democratic Art—Extension of the spheres of poetry and plastic beauty—Middle-class prejudices and pettinesses—The advent of the people—Critique of culture—America and Europe—Whitman's firm belief in Democracy—The " Divine Average "—His attitude toward the past 86

VII

Whitman's start in literature—Attempts to create a new style—Analysis of the first preface to "Leaves of Grass" (1855)—Qualities, intellectual and moral, demanded from the democratic bard 125

VIII–IX

Summary of Whitman's description of the poet—How far did he realise his own ideal?—Weak points in his method—His permanently substantial qualities—Question whether his writings are to be called poetry—Passages proving his high rank as a creative artist 139

X

Return to the difficulty of criticising Whitman—Allusive and metaphorical ways of presenting him—The main thing is to make people read him—Statement by the author of this study of what Whitman did for himself . . . 154

SHORT NOTICE OF THE LIFE OF WALT WHITMAN

WALT WHITMAN was born in the year 1819, at West Hills, on Long Island, New York State. He was the second of six sons and two daughters children of Walter Whitman and his wife, Louisa Van Velsor. The earliest known ancestor of the Whitman family was Abijah, born in England about 1560. His son, Zechariah, emigrated to Connecticut in the first half of the seventeenth century, and his grandson, Joseph, settled on Long Island. The Whitmans were probably yeomen in the old country, for I find no arms recorded under their name. The poet's mother claimed descent from one of the old Dutch families of New York.

"The Whitmans," writes Dr. Bucke, "were, and are still, a solid, tall, strong-framed, long-lived race of men, moderate of speech, friendly, fond of their land and of horses and cattle, sluggish in their passions, but fearful when once started." The Van Velsors were also farmers, occupied for the most part with horse-breeding. Walt inherited on both sides a sound constitution, untainted blood, comeliness of person, well-balanced emotions, and excellent moral principles.

Long Island, or Panmanok, as Walt loved to call it, using its ancient Indian name, is about a hundred miles in length, and has been described in these words : " Shaped like a fish, plenty of sea-shore, the horizon boundless, the air fresh and healthy, the numerous bays and creeks swarming with aquatic birds, the south-side meadows covered with salt hay, the soil generally tough, but affording numberless springs of the sweetest water in the world."

Whitman's " Leaves of Grass " are saturated through and through with the inspirations and associations of his breezy birthplace. Yet the greater portion of his early boyhood was spent at Brooklyn, whither his father, a carpenter by trade, removed. He went to school until the age of thirteen, and was then sent to learn printing. It appears, however, that Walt paid frequent visits to his relatives upon the Island. As early as

WALT WHITMAN'S BIRTHPLACE

WEST HILLS, LONG ISLAND.

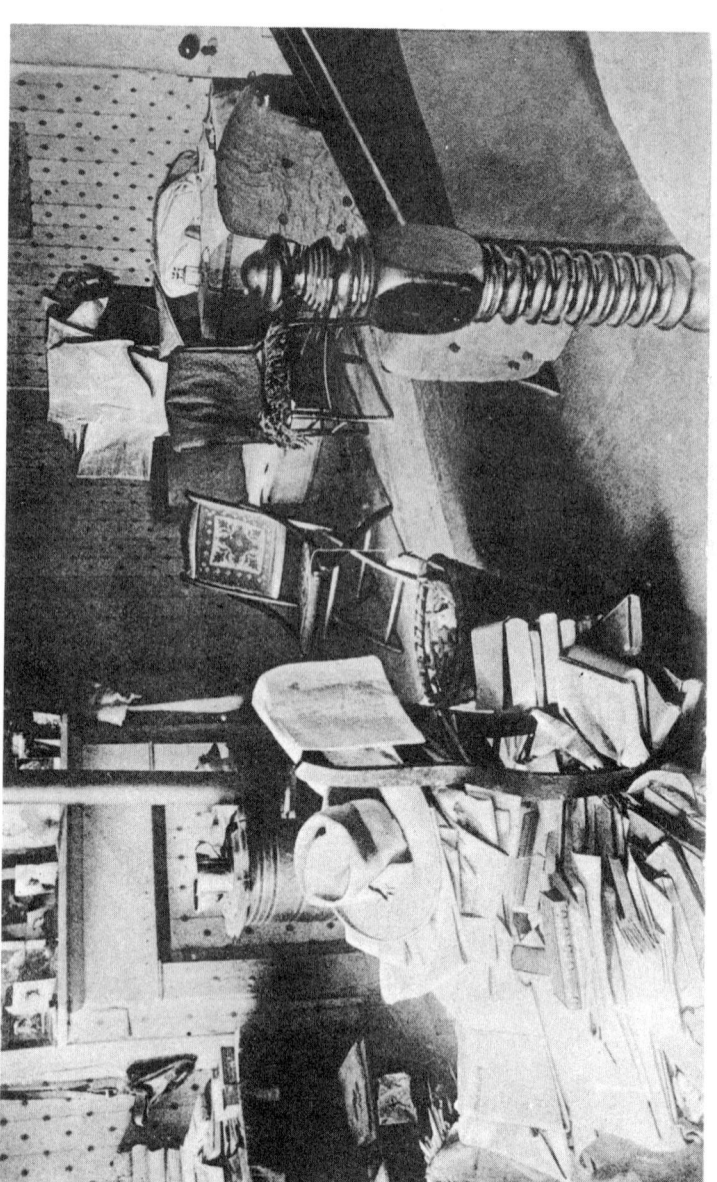

WALT WHITMAN'S ROOM
CAMDEN, NEW JERSEY.

sixteen, or thereabouts, he tramped the country, "teaching school," and began about this time to write for newspapers and magazines. In 1839-40 he edited a weekly journal called the *Long Islander*, at Huntingdon. Then he settled down in New York to the work of a compositor, combining this with journalism and public speaking.

The next period of fifteen years was decisive for his character as man of genius and citizen. He absorbed the whole life of New York and Brooklyn into his own nature, exploring every quarter of the huge city, becoming acquainted with all trades, consorting familiarly with all classes and sorts of people. The enormous variety of knowledge, the broad sympathies, the just perception of relative values in life, and the serene wisdom which distinguish "Leaves of Grass," were gained at this time. It may be well, before continuing this biographic sketch, to introduce here some descriptions of the man and his appearance, the impressions he made on friends and strangers, which have been preserved for us by those who knew him.

"Walt Whitman had a small printing-office and book-store in Myrtle Avenue, Brooklyn, where after his return from the South he started the *Freeman* newspaper, first as weekly, then as daily, and continued it a year or so. The superficial opinion about him was that he was somewhat of an idler, 'a loafer,' but not in a bad sense. He always earned his own living. I thought him a very natural person. He wore plain, cheap clothes, which were always particularly clean. Everybody knew him, every one almost liked him. We all of us (referring to the other members of his family, brothers, sisters, father and mother), long before he published 'Leaves of Grass,' looked upon him as a man who was to make a mark in the world. He was always a good listener, the best I ever knew—of late years, I think, he talks somewhat more—in those early years (1849–'54) he talked very little indeed. When he did talk his conversation was remarkably pointed, attractive, and clear. When 'Leaves of Grass' first appeared I thought it a great work, but that the man was greater than the book. His singular coolness was an especial feature. I have never seen him excited in the least degree: never heard him swear but once. He was quite grey at thirty.

He had a look of age in his youth, as he has now a look of youth in his age."

"Walt's appearance used to attract great attention from the passengers when he came on board the boat. He was quite six feet in height with the frame of a gladiator, a flowing grey beard mingled with the hairs on his broad, slightly bared chest. In his well-laundried checked shirt-sleeves, with trousers frequently pushed into his boot-legs, his fine head covered with an immense slouch black or light felt hat, he would walk about with a naturally majestic stride, a massive model of ease and independence. I hardly think his style of dress in those days was meant to be eccentric; he was very antagonistic to all show or sham, and I fancy he merely attired himself in what was handy, clean, economical, and comfortable. His marked appearance, however, obtained for him a variety of callings in the minds of passengers who did not know him. 'Is he a retired sea captain?' some would ask; 'an actor? a military officer? a clergyman? Had he been a smuggler, or in the slave trade?' To amuse Walt I frequently repeated these odd speculations upon him. He laughed until the tears ran when

I once told him that a very confidential observer had assured me he was crazy!"

"On Pennsylvania Avenue or Seventh or Fourteenth Street, or perhaps of a Sunday along the suburban road towards Rock Creek, or across on Arlington Heights, or up the shores of the Potomac, you will meet moving along at a firm but moderate pace, a robust figure, six feet high, costumed in blue or grey, with drab hat, broad shirt collar, grey-white beard, full and curly, with face like a red apple, blue eyes, and a look of animal health more indicative of hunting or boating than the department office or author's desk. Indeed, the subject of our item, in his verse, his manners, and even in his philosophy, evidently draws from, and has reference to, the influences of sea and sky, and woods and prairies, with their laws, and man in his relations to them, while neither the conventional parlour nor library has cast its spells upon him."

"Walt Whitman's dress was always extremely plain. He usually wore in pleasant weather a light-grey suit of good woollen cloth. The only thing peculiar about his dress was that he had no necktie at any time, and always wore shirts with very large turn-down collars, the button at the neck some five or six inches lower than usual, so that the throat and upper part of the breast were exposed. In all other respects he dressed in a substantial, neat, plain, common way. Everything he wore, and everything about him, was always scrupulously clean. His clothes might (and often did) show signs of wear, or they might be torn or have holes worn in them; but they never looked soiled. Indeed, an exquisite aroma of cleanliness has always been one of the special features of the man; it has always belonged to his clothes, his breath, his whole body, his eating and drinking, his conversation, and no one could know him for an hour without seeing that it penetrated his mind and life, and was in fact the expression of a purity which was physical as much as moral, and moral as much as physical."

"Lethargic during an interview, passive and receptive, an admirable listener, never in a hurry, with the air of one who has plenty of leisure, always in perfect repose, simple and direct in manners, a lover of plain, common people, 'meeter of savage and gentlemen on equal terms,' temperate, chaste, sweet-breath'd, tender and affectionate, of copious friendship, with a large, summery, paternal soul that shines in all ways and looks, he is by no means the 'rough' certain people have been so willing to believe. Fastidious as a high caste Brahmin in his food and personal neatness and cleanliness, well dressed, with a grey, open throat, a deep sympathetic voice, a kind, genial look, the impression he makes upon you is that of the best blood and breeding. He reminds one of the first men, the beginners; has a primitive outdoor look—not so much from being in the open air as from the texture and quality of his make—a look as of the earth, the sea, or the mountains, and 'is usually taken,' says a late champion of his cause, 'for some great mechanic, or stevedore, or seaman, or grand labourer of one kind or another.' His physiognomy presents very marked features—features of the true antique pattern, almost obsolete in modern faces—seen in the strong, square bridge of his nose, his high arching brows, and the absence of all bulging in his forehead—a face approximating in type to the statued Greek. He does not mean intellect merely, but life; and one feels that he must arrive at his results rather by sympathy and absorption than by hard intellectual processes—by the effluence of power rather than by direct and total application of it."

"For years past, thousands of people in New York, in Brooklyn, in Boston, in New Orleans, and latterly in Washington, have seen, even as I saw two hours ago, tallying, one might say, the streets of our American cities, and fit to have for his background and accessories their streaming populations and ample and rich façades, a man of striking masculine beauty—a poet—powerful and venerable in appearance; large, calm, superbly formed; oftenest clad in the careless, rough, and always picturesque costume of the common people; resembling, and generally taken by strangers for some great mechanic or stevedore, or seaman, or grand labourer of one kind or another; and passing slowly in this guise, with nonchalant and haughty step along the pavement, with the sunlight and shadows falling around him. The dark sombrero he usually wears was, when I saw him just now, the day being warm, held for the moment in his hand; rich light an artist would have chosen, lay upon his uncovered head, majestic, large, Homeric, and set upon his strong shoulders with the grandeur of ancient sculpture. I marked the countenance, serene, proud, cheerful, florid, grave; the brow seamed with noble wrinkles; the features massive and handsome, with firm blue eyes; the eyebrows and eyelids especially showing that fulness of arch seldom seen save in the antique busts; the flowing hair and fleecy beard, both very grey, and tempering with a look of age the youthful aspect of one who is but forty-five; the simplicity and purity of his dress cheap and plain, but spotless, from snowy falling collar to burnished boot, and exhaling faint fragrance; the whole form surrounded with manliness as with a nimbus, and breathing, in its perfect health and vigour, the august charm of the strong."

These notices are culled from various sources.* The repetition of the same points in them is the strongest evidence of Whitman's remarkable personality. His health in early manhood seems to have been absolutely perfect, and mere existence was perpetual joy.

In 1847-48 he edited the *Daily Eagle* newspaper at Brooklyn, and in 1849 he set forth on

* See Dr. Bucke's "Life of Walt Whitman," pp. 25, 33, 43, 50, 57, 99.

an excursion through the middle, southern, and western States. "He passed slowly," says Dr. Bucke, "through Pennsylvania and Virginia, crossed the Alleghany Mountains, took a steamboat at Wheeling, descended by leisurely stages the Ohio and Mississippi rivers to New Orleans, and lived there some time, employed editorially on a newspaper, the *Crescent.*" On his return journey, he took a different route, reaching New York by way of St. Louis, Chicago, Milwaukee, Detroit, the great Lakes, and Niagara. Referring to these wanderings in a letter which he empowered me to publish (dated August 19, 1890), Whitman says: "My life, young manhood, mid-age, times south, &c., have been jolly bodily, and doubtless open to criticism." After this sentence there follow details concerning his domestic circumstances, which prove that, although he never married, his youth and manhood were not passed without episodes of passion and permanent attachment.

It must be remembered that Whitman depended on labour for his bread. All through these journeyings, then, he was brought into immediate contact with the people. The United

States, in their breadth and length and largeness, became known to him, and he laid ample foundations of experience for the work of his prime.

Settling down again at Brooklyn in 1851 he edited a newspaper called the *Freeman*, and also began to build and sell houses. That proved, commercially, a paying speculation. But Walt already felt that he had something different to do in life than to make money. "Leaves of Grass" was taking shape, and of this work he says in the letter to myself already quoted: "The writing and rounding off of 'Leaves of Grass' has been to me reason-for-being and life's comfort below all." Some years elapsed before he determined upon the form which this book should assume. He made many experiments, wrote and re-wrote, testing his compositions by comparison with open nature, until at last he shaped that peculiar style which has been the subject of so much criticism.

In 1855 the first edition appeared at Brooklyn, a thin quarto volume, containing twelve poems and the prose-preface, which ranks among his most poetical performances. Whitman assisted

WALT WHITMAN ON THE WHARF
AT CAMDEN, NEW JERSEY, JULY 1890.

> Camden New Jersey — U S America
> March 30 evn'g '91 — Nothing special to write ab't — but thet I w'd forward you a line — Still keep the fort (sort o') & have had a grim winter — but signs of spring opening — have the good photos you sent me on my wall here, & y'r last Essays handy — am reading you, and not forgotten — am reading Symonds' proofs of very little 2d annex (concluding L of G.) shall send you soon as printed — God bless you
> Walt Whitman

FACSIMILE OF A POST-CARD SENT TO THE AUTHOR
AT DAVOS PLATZ FROM CAMDEN NEW JERSEY MARCH 31 1891.

at the printing of the book. It was greeted with howls of execration and roars of laughter. "When the book aroused such a tempest of anger and condemnation everywhere," he told a friend, "I went off to the east end of Long Island, and spent the late summer and all the fall—the happiest of my life—around Shelter Island and Peconic Bay. Then came back to New York with the confirmed resolution, from which I never afterwards wavered, to go on with my poetic enterprise in my own way, and finish it as well as I could." The rest of his life is inextricably interwoven with the "writing and rounding-off of 'Leaves of Grass.'" Edition following edition, at irregular intervals, between 1855 and 1892, added form and substance to the nucleus of the first twelve poems. What is most remarkable in the history of this work is the way in which the original conception admitted of infinite extension and adjustment. You feel, on looking through the slender volume of 1855, that the author already contemplated additions, and that the extremely singular style and form of his poems were adapted to this method of treatment. The growth of "Leaves of Grass" might fancifully be compared to that of a stag's antlers, which put forth yearly snags or prongs, until the stag of ten attains the fulness of majestic maturity.

Among other eminent men to whom Whitman addressed a copy of "Leaves of Grass" was Emerson. He replied in a private letter of great cordiality, which he never afterwards retracted or modified, even though Whitman and his printers adopted the rather questionable measure of publishing it in the enlarged edition of 1856. It must be inserted here, for the part this letter played in the history of Whitman's fame was important.

"CONCORD, MASS., *July* 21, 1885.

"DEAR SIR,—I am not blind to the worth of the wonderful gift of 'Leaves of Grass.' I find it the most extraordinary piece of wit and wisdom that America has yet contributed. I am very happy in reading it, as great power makes us happy. It meets the demand I am always making of what seems the sterile and stingy Nature, as if too much handiwork or too much lymph in the temperament were making our

Western wits fat and mean. I give you joy of your free and brave thought. I have great joy in it. I find incomparable things, said incomparably well, as they must be. I find the courage of treatment which so delights us, and which large perception only can inspire.

"I greet you at the beginning of a great career, which yet must have had a long foreground somewhere, for such a start. I rubbed my eyes a little, to see if this sunbeam were no illusion; but the solid sense of the book is a sober certainty. It has the best merits—namely, of fortifying and encouraging.

"I did not know, until I last night saw the book advertised in a newspaper, that I could trust the name as real and available for a post-office.

"I wish to see my benefactor, and have felt much like striking my tasks, and visiting New York to pay you my respects.

"R. W. EMERSON."

Emerson, I may add, sent a copy of "Leaves of Grass" to Carlyle, and presented one to Arthur Hugh Clough. Thoreau also began to take notice of Whitman. He was puzzled by the poet's audacities. "There are two or three pieces in the book which are disagreeable, to say the least; simply sensual." But he adds: "I do not believe that all the sermons, so-called, that have been preached in this land put together are equal to it for preaching. We ought to rejoice greatly in him." It was Thoreau, too, who said "He *is* Democracy." And here I may recall President Lincoln's remark on seeing Whitman from the windows of the White House: "Well, he *is* a MAN." Napoleon, it may be remembered, said the like to Goethe.

But the public were not of the same opinion as Emerson, Thoreau, Lincoln. The fury roused by the edition of 1856 frightened Whitman's publishers, who refused to sell the book. He meanwhile continued to compose chants in the same triumphant tone of self-complacent egotism, until he had enough new material to produce the enlarged and beautifully printed edition of 1860.

If Walt had written nothing after this, his immortality as poet would have been secured, and his thoughts in their mass and detail would have been adequately expressed. Among the most important matter added in the 1860 edition was the section entitled " Calamus."

Copies soon found their way to England, and within the space of a few years, we were all reading and discussing Walt.

Walt's life as a creative poet was rudely interrupted by the national convulsion of the great Secession War. What happened to him at that period, determined his subsequent career; partly by condemning him to the long and tedious illness, which checked his marvellous vitality at its hightide; partly by supplying him with themes for the sweetest and purest, if not the most impressive, of his poems; partly by consecrating and ennobling a personality which the public hitherto misunderstood. This does not mean that Whitman needed purification or rehabilitation on account of anything that he had previously said, or done, or published. He remained the same man, followed the track traced out at the beginning of his poet's life, abated no jot or tittle of the doctrine he felt called on to deliver. But his life during the war, his service in the cause of sufferers, his practical exemplification of principles in circumstances trying to the sturdiest and the bravest, the sacrifice of his health, the test of his religion by unwearied acts of love and charity and comradeship, forced society to recognise the essential worth and dignity of the poet, who had been condemned as a New York rowdy, a free lover, a disseminator of lawless and immoral paradoxes. No one, however prejudiced, can study *Specimen Days*—the unaffected and spontaneous record of his experience—without feeling that the grounds of common hostility to the author of *Children of Adam* must be overhauled and reconsidered. Disciples of his doctrine appeal with confidence to those pages, and say: the man who lived and acted thus, was sound to the core and worthy of a patient hearing.

How this came about, may be briefly related. Walt's brother George volunteered for the army of the north, and was wounded in the first Fredericksburg battle, December 1862. Walt started for the camp upon the Rappahannock, nursed his brother through, and then went down to Washington in charge of wounded Brooklyn soldiers. There he stayed, as an attendant in the military hospitals, bestowing the same care on men of both sides, and visiting the battle-fields.

A superficial description of his energy would profit little. Those who wish to be informed, must interrogate the original sources, which may be briefly designated the gospel of Walt Whitman's life.* For the rest, it is enough to say that constant attendance upon soldiers suffering from horrible wounds, gangrene, typhus, in those crowded hospitals, undermined his magnificent constitution. He had a serious illness in 1864, recovered from it, and returned to his work at Washington. But the seeds of permanent disease had been sown. In February 1873, he was attacked by paralysis. During the next three years, his life hung on a thread, and the man, who had been so superbly vigorous, was now condemned to invalidism. We who have been privileged to read his private correspondence at this period, know with what continued cheerfulness and courage he sustained these trials. The public has access to notes published in his complete works.† The sweetness of his nature, his sympathy for others, his affectionateness, and the sanguine faith which was his

---

* See Dr. Bucke's biography pp. 34-40, and "Specimen Days" (collected works of Walt Whitman 1888), from p. 21 to p. 80.

† "Specimen Days," after p. 80.

piety, were never altered. Poverty came to make the situation still more serious. Yet the real beauty and goodness of the man never shone more clearly than in those overclouded days. Whitman did not make a full recovery. His life dragged on a broken wing until its close in 1892. But the last twenty years of his existence on the earth were not wasted. They stamped his work as poet and prophet with the seal of indubitable genuineness. Would that all prophets, of Chelsea or otherwhere, could boast a practical commentary so efficient and illuminative of their teaching.

The poetical outcome of Walt's experience in the Secession War was a book called "Drum Taps," which appeared in 1865, including the finest of his literary efforts, that "Lament for Lincoln," which opens with the phrase, "When lilacs last in the door-yard bloomed." All these pieces have been incorporated into the later editions of "Leaves of Grass." The patriotic eloquence of Whitman's masterpiece in prose, "Democratic Vistas" (1871), obviously springs from the deepened and heightened emotions stirred in him by the awful struggle he had witnessed.

Before the end of the war Whitman received a clerkship in the Department of the Interior at Washington. Soon after this appointment the Chief Secretary, Mr. James Harlan, discharged him, "because he was the author of an indecent book." Mr. Harlan, it appears, had used his liberty as chief of this State office to inspect his clerk's desk, and found in it an annotated copy of "Leaves of Grass." That happened in the summer of 1865. Nine weeks after the event, Mr. William Douglas O'Connor, of Washington, who had learned to appreciate Walt as a friend, and to admire him as a writer, appeared before the public with a vindication of the "Good Gray Poet." The attack on Secretary Harlan was scathing, the rhetoric tremendous. And in 1883 Mr. O'Connor returned to the assault with fiercer animosity, and still more copious eloquence.*
Now that Whitman is lying cold and still beneath the huge block of granite at Camden, we need not rake up the embers of that volcanic controversy. There are confessedly passages in "Leaves of Grass" which offend the ordinary

* Both pieces are published in Dr. Bucke's "Life of Walt Whitman," pp. 71–132.

sense of propriety, and opinions on such points admit of difference. The fact, however, remains that the book in question was out of print at the time of Harlan's action, and did not reappear until the year 1867. Meanwhile Whitman had obtained another clerkship in the office of the Attorney-General at Washington. This, too, he lost in the summer of 1874, when he was ill and incapacitated from active service by paralysis at Camden. I have before me copies of letters written to a dear friend at the time. They show a serene indifference to the disaster, and a tranquil outlook over the immediate future. And yet no source of income remained to him. "Leaves of Grass" was not what publishers would call a "property." The book brought in next to nothing. How Whitman bore the accumulated troubles of that period has been so well set forth by his friend Dr. Bucke, that I cannot omit the passage:

"As to the profits of 'Leaves of Grass,' they had never been much, and now two men, in succession, in New York (T. O'K. and C. P. S.), in whose hands the sale of the book, on commission, had been placed, took advantage of his helplessness to embezzle the amounts due (they calculated that death would soon settle the score and rub it out). So that, although I hardly ever heard him speak of them, I know that during those four years Walt Whitman had to bear the imminent prospect of death, great pain and suffering at times, poverty, his poetic enterprise a failure, and the face of the public either clouded in contempt or turned away with indifference. If a man can go through such a trial as this without despair or misanthropy—if he can maintain a good heart, can preserve absolute self-respect, and as absolutely the respect, love, and admiration of the few who thoroughly know him —then he has given proofs I should say of personal heroism of the first order. It was, perhaps, needed that Walt Whitman should afford such proofs; at all events he has afforded them. What he was, how he lived, kept himself up during those years, and how at the end partially recuperated, is so well set forth by himself in 'Specimen Days,' that it would be mere impertinence for any one else to attempt to retell the tale. The illness his friends looked upon with so much dread has borne fruit in one of the sanest

and sweetest of books, the brightest and halest
'Diary of an Invalid' ever written—a book
unique in being the expression of strength in
infirmity—the wisdom of weakness—so bright
and translucent, at once of the earth earthy, and
spiritual as of the sky and stars. Other books
of the invalid's room require to be read with
the blinds drawn down and the priest on the
threshold; but this sick man's chamber is the
lane, and by the creek or sea-shore—always
with the fresh air and the open sky overhead."

Little more is left to be related. Whitman's
father died in the year 1855; his mother died at
Camden (New Jersey) in 1873. To this town
Whitman came during the first months of his
paralytic seizure. And here he remained till
his own death in March 1892. His last years
were cheered and comforted by the devoted
attention of many friends, among whom Dr.
R. M. Bucke and Mr. Horace Traubel, John
Burroughs and Mrs. Gilchrist, F. Warren Fritzinger and Mrs. Davis ought to be especially
commemorated. He had the satisfaction of
feeling that "Leaves of Grass" at last was
making way. It had been partially re-issued

in England by W. M. Rossetti, and an English school of hearty admirers grew up in Lancashire. Selections were translated into German by Karl Knortz and T. W. Rolleston. French critics devoted serious studies to its literary qualities and philosophical teaching.* And what was better than fame, affection of the strongest, tenderest, and purest quality attended him from staunch and noble men whom he could love and honour. His work lives after him. It is of a kind which the world will not willingly let die.

* While correcting these proofs, I notice that a literary Society at Padua is going at their next meeting to discuss " the poem of Walt Whitman" (Venice, March 20, 1893).

A STUDY OF WALT WHITMAN

I

The world has lost another good and great man. Walt Whitman died in March 1892 at Camden, New Jersey, U.S.A., after a lingering and painful illness, which terminated in distressing debility, borne by him with serenity and fortitude. A spiritual force has been resumed through his death into the occult stock of universal energy; and it is too early as yet to sum up any final account of his achievement as the teacher of a new way of regarding life, the prophet of a democratic religion, and the poet of a revolutionary school.

Whitman, indeed, is extremely baffling to criticism. I have already said in print that "speaking about him is like speaking about the universe." I meant this to be appreciative, in so far as the largeness and comprehensiveness of the man's nature are concerned. But the saying has, like the famous Delphian knife, a double handle. Not merely because he is large and comprehensive, but because he is intangible, elusive, at first sight self-contradictory, and in some sense formless, does Whitman resemble the universe and defy critical analysis.

The peculiar surroundings of the man during his lifetime rendered it difficult to be impartial with regard to him. Assuming from the first an attitude of indifference to public opinion, challenging conventionalities, and quietly ignoring customary prejudice, he was exposed at the beginning of his career to unmerited insults and a petty persecution. Not only did critics and cultivated persons fling stones at him; but even a Minister of State thought it his duty to deprive him of a modest office which he held. This opposition was far from abating his courage or altering the calm of his essentially masculine nature. But it excited the pugnacious instincts of those few devoted followers and disciples who had gathered round him. Whitman began to be enveloped in a dust of controversy—indecent abuse upon the one hand, extravagant laudation on the other—outrage and depreciation, retaliated by what the French call *réclame* and *claque*. Sane criticism found it necessary to stand aloof from the ignoble fray; feeling confident that Whitman's worth would obtain due and ultimate recognition; knowing, as Sam Johnson used to say, that "no man is written up or down except by himself"; dreading lest the sterling qualities of such magnificent work should be brought into discredit by clamorous and undiscriminating advocacy.

Whitman's own personality augmented these difficulties. No one was ever more generous and frank of nature, more ready to accept differences of opinion, more tolerant of criticism. At the same time he displayed a desire to diffuse his doctrines, an eagerness to be acknowledged in his lifetime. He craved for responsive affection in the audience to whom he appealed, and regarded his literary teaching in the light of a cause. He acted like one who did not trust to the certainty of the eventual success of genius. He collected and distributed trifling panegyrics of himself, culled from the holes and corners of

American journalism. He showed small sense of proportion in criticism, and seemed to value people by the amount of personal zeal they displayed in the propagation of his views. This spirit was somewhat grotesquely exhibited in his table-talk at a banquet held in honour of his seventy-second birthday.* The kindness of his words about his friends and followers must have touched all who were concerned, as much, I hope, as they touched me. When I read what he said of me, I recognised the acumen of his insight into several points of my character. I felt that probably my name would survive in those unpremeditated remarks long after my own writings shall have been forgotten. Yet I could not help being amused by one sentence, which gave a special flavour to his praise : " The best thing about Symonds is his splendid aspiration. He was quite willing to leap into the gulf." Whitman, as the context proves, did not mean that Symonds is a Quintus Curtius, open to undertake a job of self-devotion at a moment's notice. He was only testing me by the standard

* *See* Walt Whitman's Birthday, May 31, 1891, *Lippincott's Magazine.*

of discipleship, which he applied to each and all of his acquaintances in turn. Early in the history of "Leaves of Grass" I accepted the book, and staked my critical reputation upon an open avowal of its sterling merit—indifferent to what my brother-students thought about it. That is no topic for eulogy: certainly none which need have been dwelt upon by Whitman. It may be false delicacy, it may be the result of effete culture, it may be feudalism in my blood. But I confess that I have always found this note in Whitman and his circle difficult to keep in tune with.

As Ernest Renan said of Victor Hugo, writing on the day after his death: " Who would now interrogate the general upon the subject of the manœuvres he employed, the sacrifices which were the conditions of his success ? The general is forced to be egotistic. He is the army; and a glaring exhibition of personality, unpardonable in the rest of men, is imposed on him by circumstances. Hugo (*and in like manner Whitman*) had become a symbol, a principle, an affirmation, the affirmation of idealism and emancipated art. He owed the whole of himself to his own religion.

He was like a god, who had to be his own high priest. His lofty and vigorous nature lent itself to the playing of this part, which would have been unbearable to one of different calibre. A mighty instinct came to manifestation through him. He was like the main-spring of a spiritual world. He could not find the time to have taste; good taste, moreover, would have been of little service to him." There is irony in everything which Renan wrote; and these sentences (transferred by me from his panegyric of Hugo to Whitman) are steeped in irony. To dispense with taste, or the refinements of gentle feelings, is what no man, not even the greatest, can do with impunity. No general, not even Napoleon, no founder, not even Christ was great enough for that. Whitman then appeared omnivorous of praise, indiscriminative as to its quality, lacking the repose which belongs to the highest type of greatness. Instead of leaving his fame and influence to the operation of natural laws, he encouraged the *claque* and the *réclame* which I have pointed out as prejudicial.

I sincerely regard him, and have long regarded him, as a man born to remind the world of many important and neglected truths, to flash the light of authentic inspiration upon many dark and puzzling questions, and to do so with the force of admirable courage, flawless candour. But the ways he chose for pushing his gospel and advertising his philosophy, put a severe strain on patience. Were Buddha, Socrates, Christ, so interested in the dust stirred up around them by second-rate persons, in third-rate cities, and in more than fifth-rate literature ?

In addition to what I have been advancing upon the difficulty of dealing fairly with Whitman during his lifetime—passing now to higher and more serious planes of reflection—his very originality, his individuality, the unique qualities which made him so remarkable a master, render the task of seizing and formulating the essential truth about him, both as teacher and as poet, well-nigh impracticable at the present time. Those of us who feel his influence most deeply, believe that his work has secured attention, and hope ardently that its import will be gradually absorbed and assimilated, so that in course of time a living image of himself shall exist in thousands, and the exposition be rendered easy.

Like Nature, he seemed, at first sight, to be a mass of contradictions and insoluble problems, of potent stuffs irreducible by any known method of analysis. We could feel him, submit to his impact, be enamoured of his charm. But we knew that it was impossible to find a formula for all that is implied in the two letters W. W. Critics, saddened, and made shy by their thankless task, judged it better to leave him to his predestined working in the sphere of thought, feeling assured that, like Nature, he could take care of himself.

How ill it fared with even superior intelligences in their efforts to evaluate W. W. might be illustrated by two examples. When " Songs before Sunrise " were re-issued in 1883, Mr. Swinburne suffered an eloquent ode " To Walt Whitman in America " to be reprinted. It contains the following impassioned stanza :

> O strong-winged soul with prophetic
>   Lips hot with the bloodbeats of song,
> With tremor of heartstrings magnetic,
>   With thoughts as thunders in throng,
> With consonant ardours of chords
> That pierce men's souls as with swords
>   And hale them hearing along.

On reading this ode, and especially the lines just quoted, I, for my part, felt that true things had here been said regarding Whitman, but with rather more of the *claque* and the *réclame* flavour than I judged desirable. Still, I welcomed and appreciated the poem as a noteworthy contribution to the tradition gradually forming in support of Whitman's credit. Sad then was my disappointment to discover, before the eighties were over (that is within seven years of this dithyrambic blessing), that Mr. Swinburne was cursing Whitman by all his gods in prose, and stigmatising the muse of " Leaves of Grass," as a drunken apple-woman reeling in a gutter. I forget the exact verbiage of the scurrility; and I do not impute the change of attitude implied in it, so much to Mr. Swinburne's levity, as to the bewilderment created in his mind by Whitman's incongruities.

The next instance is that of a critic not so lavish of the hyperboles of praise and blame as Mr. Swinburne is. My friend Mr. R. L. Stevenson once published a constrained and measured study of Walt Whitman, which struck some of those who read it as frigidly appreciative. He subsequently told me that he had first opened upon the key-note of a glowing panegyric, but felt the pompous absurdity of its exaggeration. He began again, subduing the whole tone of the composition. When the essay was finished in this second style, he became conscious that it misrepresented his own enthusiasm for the teacher who at a critical moment of his youthful life had helped him to discover the right line of conduct.

I feel that I may not unfairly be accused by the school of Whitman of having been lukewarm toward him in his lifetime, and of having started this memorial notice in a somewhat carping strain. Here, as elsewhere, however, it is my single desire to live in the Whole, and to see things, so far as may be possible, in their relation to the Whole. I am sure, moreover, that Whitman's genial and manly spirit, so lately resumed into the sum of things, approves of any earnest attempt on his disciple's part to show what his relative value is. No one, not Buddha, not Socrates, not Christ, has an absolute value. True criticism dares not forget that "the eternal things," "the abiding relations" of the universe, extend around, above us all, sustaining and environing individualities however potent.

In 1889 I allowed the following words of mine to be circulated in a collection of what may be called testimonials to the bard of Camden: " 'Leaves of Grass,' which I first read at the age of twenty-five, influenced me more perhaps than any other book has done, except the Bible; more than Plato, more than Goethe. It is impossible for me to speak critically of what has so deeply entered into the fibre and marrow of my being."

The time has now come for attempting some explanation of what I meant. Whitman threw clear light upon truths which I had but dimly perceived, and gave me the courage of opinions previously held with some timidity and shyness.

I will try to express his influence under several headings. It should, however, be premised that Whitman does not lend himself to systematic exposition.

He says emphatically:

I charge you, too, for ever, reject those who would expound
  me—for I cannot expound myself;
I charge you that there be no theory or school founded out
  of me;
I charge you to leave all free, as I have left all free.

It is useless to extract a coherent scheme of thought from his voluminous writings. He tells us himself that he is full of contradictions, that his precepts will do as much harm as good, that he desires to " tally the broadcast doings of the day and the night." But though he may not be reducible to system, we can trace an order in his ideas. First comes religion or the concept of the universe ; then personality, or the sense of self and sex ; then love, diverging into the amative and comradely emotions ; then democracy, or the theory of human equality and brotherhood. The world, man as an essential part of the world, man as of prime importance to himself alone, love and liberty as necessary to his happiness ; these are the constituents of Whitman's creed,

II

I will take Religion first. Ernest Renan, in the paper from which I have quoted, written immediately after Victor Hugo's death, uttered some remarks about the central thought of that great poet, which may be used as text and introduction for what I have to say about Walt Whitman. "Is he spiritualist? Is he materialist? I remain in ignorance. Upon the one side, he does not know what abstraction is. His principal devotion, I might say the only one, is for two or three eminent realities, such as Paris, Napoleon, the People. Concerning souls, he abides by the same conception as Tertullian's. He believes that he can see them, touch them. Immortality, in his idea, is not the mere immortality of thought. At the same time he is in the highest degree an idealist. The idea, for him, penetrates matter, constitutes the essence and the reason of its being.

His God is not the God concealed of Spinoza, foreign to the evolution of the universe; it is a God to whom it may be useless to address prayer, but whom he worshipped with a kind of trembling. It is the abysm of the Gnostics. His life was passed under the puissant preoccupation of a living infinite, which embraced him, surged around and from him on all sides and portions of his being, and in the bosom of which it was sweet to him to lose himself and lose his reason."

Here we have a fine description of a great spirit, which offered analogies to Whitman's, but which differed in some essential particulars. By commenting upon this passage I will try to bring into relief what seems to me to have been Whitman's fundamental conception of the universe and man's relation to it—of religion in short. Whether he was a spiritualist or a materialist need no more be discussed in his case than in that of Victor Hugo. Those who conceive of cosmic unity at all, contemplate spirit and matter as the x and y of one inscrutable, yet only real, existence. This was undoubtedly the attitude of Whitman. Every detail of the world endowed with life, with shape, contained for him God, was a microcosm of the whole, an apparent and ever-recurring miracle. Upon abstractions he refused to dwell, because (without having perhaps appropriated the Hegelian philosophy) he regarded the concrete as the ultimate reality, the self-effectuation of the Idea, while the abstract remains mere gaping void. For Whitman, as for Hugo, two or three immense facts were the main objects of his enthusiasm. We may describe them as America, Self, Sex, the People. Whether Hugo really held by Tertullian's concrete notion of the soul, as Renan puts it, I will not pause to debate. Whitman certainly did not. For him Soul was the most etherealised, the least palpable and visible, yet the most formative and durable element in everything that is. He clung to the belief in immortality. Yet he never attempted to define what immortality will be. His strongest faith in the survival of the individual is expressed in phrases like these :

> My foot is tenoned and mortised in granite,
> I laugh at what you call dissolution,
> And I know the amplitude of time.

I know not how I came of you, and I know not where I go
with you; but I know I came well, and shall go well.

Whitman's God, like the God attributed to Hugo, like Goethe's God, is immanent in the universe.

> God dwells within and moves the world and moulds,
> Himself and Nature in one form enfolds;
> Thus all that lives in Him, and breathes, and is,
> Shall ne'er His puissance, ne'er His spirit miss.

Yet this God was not for him the object of trembling adoration. Rather he says:

> Me imperturbe, standing at ease in Nature.

I hear and behold God in every object, yet understand God
not in the least,
Nor do I understand who there can be more wonderful than
myself.

Nothing, not God, is greater to one than one's self is. Nor again was the supreme being the abysm of the Gnostics for his soul, but the ever present fact, which everywhere exists around us, in which we exist, which we help to constitute, nearer and more essential to us than aught else. To pray to such a God is of course useless, except in the sense of committing ourselves to him, as the bird gives itself to the air, the wave rocks upon the vast profound it ruffles, the ray of light floats undulating through illimitable ether : bird, wave, and sunbeam, just like the soul of man, being each a distinct and indispensable part of that totality in which it lives and moves and has its being.

In Whitman's thought, as in that of Bruno, Spinoza, Goethe, there is no separation of God from the Universe. Therefore what is said about the latter, holds good of the former. In spite of the reality of both to our soul, both are unknown and unknowable in their essence. The same is true of Life and Death. Therefore all forms of religions, faiths, metaphysics, cosmologies, remain in the region of mere guesses, and possess no more than a relative value for the understanding.

> I heard what was said of the universe ;
> Heard it and heard it of several thousand years;
> It is middling well as far as it goes,—but is that all ?
>
> Magnifying and applying come I,
> Outbidding at the start the old cautious hucksters,
> Taking myself the exact dimensions of Jehovah,

Lithographing Kronos, Zeus his son, and Hercules his
    grandson ;
Buying drafts of Osiris, Isis, Belus, Brahma, Buddha,
In my portfolio placing Manito loose, Allah on a leaf, the
    crucifix engraved,
With Odin, and the hideous-faced Mexitli, and every idol and
    image ;
Taking them all for what they are worth, and not a cent
    more ;
Admitting they were alive and did the work of their days;
Accepting the rough deific sketches to fill out better in my-
    self—bestowing them freely on each man and woman I see.

This passage, though it may sound irreverent, is nothing more than an expression of the belief that theology is the subject of comparative study, and has to be considered from the point of view of historical development. There is no finality in any creed, nor can there be, because man's place in the universe is but a speck of cloud in an illimitable sky, a fragment of straw afloat upon a boundless ocean. This does not prevent what Whitman calls religion—that is to say, a sturdy confidence in the security of the whole scheme of things, a sense of universal life and of our indestructible participation in the same—from being for him the most important of all human facts and qualities.

I say the whole earth, and all the stars in the sky, are for
    Religion's sake.

I say no man has ever yet been half devout enough,
None has ever yet adored or worshipped half enough,
None has begun to think how divine he himself is, or how
    certain the future is.

I say that the real and permanent grandeur of These States
    must be their religion ;
Otherwise there is no real and permanent grandeur ;
(Nor character, nor life worthy the name, without Religion ;
Nor land, nor man or woman, without Religion).

The Religion of which he speaks might be defined as a recognition of divinity in all things. It is a profound belief in the eternity of Spirit underlying all appearances, phenomena, transitions of birth and death, development, and dissolution. Its essence is an imperturbable optimism, or what he elsewhere designates as "unrestricted faith." No apparent irrationality or contradictions in the world as we perceive it, ought to shake this faith. The origin of evil offers no problem. If God, as you theologians aver, made the world, then God made evil as well as good. There is no way of extricating yourselves from the corollaries of your own theorem. You say, indeed, that God made the world out of nothing; and that, having made it, God remains apart from it and independent. But what do you mean by nothing, when there can be nothing at all but God? It is impossible to conceive of God in any way, least of all in the way which your metaphysic forces on the human mind, and at the same time to conceive of something which is not a part of God. Therefore God made the world out of himself, or rather he is the world; and everything in the world, what we call bad as well as what we call good, the ugly as well as the beautiful to our eyes, the painful as well as the pleasurable to our senses, is God. There is no possible method of eluding this argument, unless you posit matter as outside God and independent of him, in which case the Universe contains two Gods. But that is what you theologians are anxious to deny.

It must not be imagined that Whitman uses this language. On the contrary, he says to mankind :

> Be not curious about God,
> For I, who am curious about each, am not curious about God.

A STUDY OF WALT WHITMAN

He refuses to discuss and formulate what he feels to be in everything around him.

Why should I wish to see God better than this day?
I see something of God each hour of the twenty-four, and each moment then;
In the faces of men and women I see God, and in my own face in the glass;
I find letters from God drop't in the street—and every one is sign'd by God's name,
And I leave them where they are, for I know that wheresoe'er I go,
Others will punctually come for ever and ever.

But, though he does not employ irrefutable arguments against orthodox theology, these are implied in the position of unrestricted faith and imperturbable optimism which he assumes. In like manner, though he will not argue with materialism, he says to modern science : All your theories of the universe lead inevitably to the conclusion that one spiritual vitality pervades the whole. The world, as you present it to our reason, must be thought, because we think the world, because the order of the world is uniform, intelligible to our understanding, progressing by ascertainable processes of evolution. Everything in the world is the thought of some spirit or soul, for which the name of God is a convenient symbol.

Therefore, he is able to proclaim :

I make the poem of evil also—I commemorate that part also.

I am myself just as much evil as good, and so my nation is. And I say there is in fact no evil

(Or if there is, I say it is just as important to you, to the land, or to me, as anything else).

In strict conformity with this view of things, he includes Satan, the genius of revolt, dissatisfaction, discord, in his conception of divinity. One of his most remarkable poems, " Chanting the Square Deific," is, in fact, an analysis of the Divine Ideal; not that men may presume to describe the world-soul as it ontologically is, but that the intellect of man, anthropomorphic by the law of its own nature, imagines this to be endowed with spiritual qualities analogous to those it recognises in itself. The Square Deific is what man thinks and feels, when proceeding outward from himself, his personality, the " I " of Whitman's fundamental creed, he formulates his impressions of the universal spirit. The Square is not Deity, because we can predicate nothing about God. It is Deific, or God-making, because we are compelled to make God in our image.

This poem is so important for the understanding of Whitman's thought that we must examine it more closely. What then, are the four main conceptions which he considers necessary to the Divine Idea? The first is that of inexorable destiny, implacable fact. This gives birth to deities like Jehovah, Brahma, Kronos, Earth.

> I am Time, old, modern as any,
> Unpersuadable, relentless, executing righteous judgments,
> Aged beyond computation, yet ever new, ever with those mighty laws rolling,
> Relentless, I forgive no man—whoever sins dies—I will have that man's life;
> Therefore let none expect mercy. Have the seasons gravitation, the appointed days mercy? No more have I,
> But as the seasons and gravitation, and as all the appointed days that forgive not,
> I dispense from this side judgments inexorable without the least remorse.

Thus the first and fundamental side of the four-square Idea is Law, that which science demonstrates. The second conception is that of consolation, healing, affection. It creates deities like the Lord Christ, Hermes, Hercules.

Many times have I been rejected, taunted, put in prison, and
   crucified, and many times shall be again,
All the world have I given up for my dear brothers' and
   sisters' sake, for the soul's sake,
Wending my way through the homes of men, rich or poor,
   with the kiss of affection,
For I am affection, I am the cheer-bringing God, with hope
   and all-enclosing charity.

The second side of the square appears to contradict and compensate the first, yet it is no less eternal and indispensable to the idea.

But my charity has no death—my wisdom dies not, neither
   early nor late,
And my sweet love bequeathed here and elsewhere never dies.

The third conception is that of revolt, of Satan.

Aloof, dissatisfied, plotting revolt,
Comrade of criminals, brother of slaves,
Crafty, despised, a drudge, ignorant,
With Sudra face and worn brow, black, but in the depths of
   my heart, proud as any,
Lifted now and always against whoever scorning assumes to
   rule me.

Satan, no less eternal, no less indispensable to the idea than Law and Charity, but seeming to contradict both, will remain " permanent here from my side, equal with any, real as any."

In other words, the human mind cannot project a spiritual world where strife shall not reign as well as love, and both be antagonistic to destiny. Charity and Hatred are alike needed for organic life. Law alone would congeal the universe into an inert crystal. But now appears the fourth conception, which, according to Whitman's feeling of the world, unites and fuses law, love, revolt in a more ethereal essence—what Shelley phrased the "Life of Life"—the true spirituality, the essential vitality of the vast complex. By a strange whim of fancy, while he adopts the Holy Ghost of Christian theology, Whitman uses the female gender. His phrase is "Santa Spirita," instead of "Sanctus Spiritus." In dealing with Whitman's language, the critic has, in such cases, either to credit him with an esoteric meaning or to suppose that he was regardless of grammar and usage. Did he intend to suggest that the Anima Mundi, which forms the fourth and resultant concept of his Square Deific, possesses an essential femininity? Was he casting a side-glance at Goethe's "Ewig-Weibliches"? I am inclined to repudiate that explanation of this "Santa

Spirita." We shall see that when he comes to treat of human loves and passions, the female is regarded as the fundamental element of sex and sexual attraction, the male as the ethereal and all pervasive element of free affection. Therefore, in the present instance, I take the phrase "Santa Spirita" to be a variation on the old theme of the Holy Ghost, introduced with sensitive æsthetic tact, but with more than an Emperor Sigismund's disregard for accidence, in order to shadow forth a frail and fugitive, but eminently vital, conception. Whitman's actual words must be repeated. Their mysticism is far too subtle for abridgment or description. He is engaged in trying once again to express what Bruno thought, what throbs in the heart of those of us who feel that Science marries with Religion—namely, that there is a point beyond Law, Love and Hatred, where the harmony we dimly guess, on which our faith is founded, merges in eternal, concrete, spiritual energy. His unrestricted faith, his imperturbable optimism, transcends the sphere of law, charity, revolt. Jehovah, Jesus, Satan, find the resolution of their discord, the atonement of their contradiction, in that unity of the universe which can only be dimly apprehended by our mortal minds, but upon which our confidence as creatures of the total scheme is fixed and grounded. He calls it "Santa Spirita." Shelley, as I noted, called it "Life of Life." Under this or that name, under any name, it connotes the individual's conviction that he is an inviolable factor of the universal order, unable to escape from its decrees, incapable of dispensing with the consolation of the heart, condemned to suffer and rebel, yet conscious that the music of the whole, if heard in its entirety by him, would justify his separate striving.

Santa Spirita, breather, life,

Beyond the light, lighter than light,

Beyond the flames of hell, joyous, leaping easily above hell,

Beyond Paradise, perfumed solely with my own perfume,

Including all life on earth, touching, including God, including Saviour and Satan,

Ethereal, pervading all, (for without me what were all? what were God?)

Essence of forms, life of the real identities, permanent, positive, (namely the unseen),

Life of the great round world, the sun and stars, and of man, I, the general soul,

Here the square finishing, the solid, I the most solid,
Breathe my breath also through these songs.

With this blast of mysticism, Whitman leaves us. But the mysticism is carefully adapted to the conditions under which we have to live; inexorable law, tender and recurrent charities, burning black-hearted no less recurrent revolts against law, heart-broken negations of love—these are our permanent visible relations to the scheme of things. But there is a fourth relation, transcending and including these, beyond them, and above them, beneath them, and embracing them, which gives the human heart the hope of final reconciliation to its destiny. Whitman, in his imperturbable optimism, his unrestricted faith, declares that this fourth and final relation is the one which souls are bound to stand by. Here we find the truth, " the solid, the most solid."

What looks ethereal and evanescent, what seems to be a dream of perfection, a vision of unrealised harmony, constitutes the pith and substance, the fibre and the soul, the irrefragable and unremovable ground-work of the whole. The most spiritual, the least tangible, the most irreducible to terms of actual experience, is the ultimate reality, unifying all things. That is what he means by soul, when speaking of the cosmos. That is the man's religion; and as such, he bids us to accept it. "By faith shall ye live."

How much or how little of a Christian Whitman was, can be judged from the foregoing extracts. In the technical sense of that word, as understood by existing Churches, he was clearly not a Christian. But if the Christianity of Christ, as apart from that of Christendom, be intended, then he fully shared its spirit. He retained a tender reverence for Jesus, whom he called "the Lord Christ," and to whom he accorded the title of "divine." It is the beauty of Christ's character, his brotherhood, his religion of love, the sacredness of his mission—a mission still capable of being imitated—it is this which enthrals the heart of the man; not the fable of his miraculous nativity, nor the Miltonic scheme of vicarious redemption.

Recall Christ, brother of rejected persons—brother of slaves, felons, idiots, and of insane and diseased persons.

Then again, it is the charm of that nomadic life in Galilee, that " sweet story of old," as the children's hymn expressed it, which attracts him.

> Walking the old hills of Judæa with the beautiful gentle God at my side.

How near to Renan's "doux Galiléen," and yet, in spirit, how far closer to the children's hymn, is that phrase! In this mood of loving comradeship with Christ, the brother of rejected persons, the sufferer for others, the gentle God, Whitman wrote that address, "To Him that was Crucified," which has been challenged for undue familiarity. In the same mood, he spoke those strong and sustaining words, "To one shortly to die," against which no cavil can be raised. In the same mood, he expressed his brotherhood for persons whom other men misuse and cast aside like pestilent rags, in the lines called "The City Dead-House." Inspired by the spirit of this Christ, he laid his health and manhood down as a willing sacrifice for the sick and wounded soldiers of the great American War. How much or how little of a real follower after Christ Whitman was, can be judged from these things.

Still, it was not Whitman's vocation or his deliberate intention to shore up tottering his-

torical Christianity in any of its dogmatic forms.
"I too," he says, in one of his apparently
egotistic proclamations; "I too, following many,
and follow'd by many, inaugurate a Religion
—I too, go to the wars." We have seen what
was the essence of that religion, its imperturbable optimism and unrestricted faith. We
might call it the Cosmic Enthusiasm, and hail
it as the dawn of a new spiritual day. But it
was not Christianity, any more than it was
Mohammedanism or Buddhism, or Græco-Roman
Paganism. It has a character and essence of
its own, from which the notions of personal
Deity, of rewards and punishments for the individual, of salvation and damnation, of heaven
and hell, have been purged away. The secret
of Whitman, his inner wisdom, consists in
attaining an attitude of confidence, a sense of
security, by depending on the great thought of
the universe, to which all things including our
particular selves are attached by an indubitable
link of vital participation. This religion corresponds exactly to the Scientific Principia of the
modern age; to the evolutionary hypothesis with
its display of an immense unfolding organism, to

the correlation of forces and the conservation of energy, which forbid the doubt of any atom wasted, any part mismade or unaccounted for eventually.

Sustained by this conception that nothing can be ultimately lost, or doomed to pain, or annihilated, in the universal frame, Whitman feels strong enough to cry :

> My foot is tenoned and mortised in granite,
> I laugh at what you call dissolution,
> And I know the amplitude of time.

In the poem of " Burial " he says :

> You are not thrown to the winds—you gather certainly and safely around yourself ;
> Yourself! Yourself! Yourself, for ever and ever.

Innumerable passages might be culled from his writings in which this sense of the immortality of self, based by him on a purely scientific conception of the universe, but inspired with the fervour of faith, bursts forth in songs of jubilation at the thought of death. Human life has had infinite antecedents, and must expect an infinite progression in the future. Millions of years do not reckon in its course. Sooner or later, it will arrive at its fulfilment. The spectacle of the stars at night cannot daunt a robust spirit with the dread of its own nothingness. On the contrary, the stars inflate his bosom with the conviction that,

There is no stoppage, and never can be stoppage;
If I, you, the world, and all beneath or upon their surfaces,
    were this moment reduced to a pallid float, it would
    not avail in the long run;
We should surely bring up again where we now stand,
And as surely go as much farther, and then farther and
    farther.

The thought of this continual progression of the universe, to what end and for what purpose no man knoweth, will for many persons be intolerable. But for Whitman it is exhilarating; it is, in other words, his religion.

My rendezvous is appointed—it is certain;
The Lord will be there, and wait till I come, on perfect terms;
(The great Camerado, the lover true for whom I pine, will
    be there).

Whether this cosmic enthusiasm, which has been expressed by Whitman with a passion of self-dedication, a particularity of knowledge, and a sublimity of imagination, unapproached by any poet-prophet since the death of Bruno, is destined to reinforce the soul of man with faith, and to inaugurate a new religion, I dare not even pause to question. We are told that it is not calculated to inspire the ignorant with rapture, to console the indigent and suffering by suggestions of some mitigation of their lot.

Still I may point out that it is the only type of faith which agrees with the conclusions and determinations of science. To bear the yoke of universal law is the plain destiny of human beings. If we could learn to bear that yoke with gladness, to thrill with vibrant fibres to the pulses of the infinite machine we constitute—(for were it possible that the least of us should be eliminated, annihilated, the whole machine would stop and crumble into chaos)—if, I say, we could feel pride and joy in our participation of the cosmic life, then we might stand where Whitman stood with "feet tenoned and mortised in granite." I do not think it is a religion only for the rich, the powerful, the wise, the healthy. For my own part, I may confess that it shone upon me when my life was broken, when I was weak, sickly, poor, and of no account; and that I have ever lived thenceforward in the light and warmth of it. In bounden duty toward Whitman, I make this personal statement; for had it not been for the contact of his fervent spirit with my own, the pyre ready to be lighted, the combustible materials of modern thought awaiting the touch of the fire-bringer, might never have leapt up into the flame of life-long faith and consolation. During my darkest hours, it comforted me with the conviction that I too played my part in the illimitable symphony of cosmic life. When I sinned, repined, sorrowed, suffered, it touched me with a gentle hand of sympathy and understanding, sustained me with the strong arm of assurance that in the end I could not go amiss (for I was part, an integrating part of the great whole); and when strength revived in me, it stirred a healthy pride and courage to effectuate myself, to bear the brunt of spiritual foes, the slings and arrows of outrageous fortune. For this reason, in duty to my master Whitman, and in the hope that my experience may encourage others to seek the same source of inspiration, I have exceeded the bounds of an analytical essay by pouring forth my personal confession.

III

THE inscription prefixed to "Leaves of Grass, opens thus :

> Small is the theme of the following Chant, yet the greatest—
> namely, ONE'S SELF—that wondrous thing, a simple,
> separate person.

In all his writings, Whitman has kept personality steadily in view, as the leading motive of his poetic and prophetic utterance. He regards wealth, material prosperity, culture, as nothing in comparison with vigorous manhood and womanhood. "The greatest city is that which has the greatest man or woman." "Nothing endures but personal qualities." "The greater the reform needed, the greater the personality you need to accomplish it" Nations, consequently, rise or fall, according to the quality of the persons who constitute them. Human beings are nothing, possess nothing, enjoy nothing, except through, and by their self, their personality. To prove this, to demonstrate what an incomparably precious thing a free and healthy personality, self-centred, self-reliant, self-effectuated, is for the owner of it, how it transcends every other possession which riches or learning can confer, becomes the first object of his teaching. Secondly, he aims at showing that nations only thrive and are strong by the character, the grit, the well-developed personality, of their inhabitants. Nothing can preserve a nation in prosperity, or perpetuate its fame, except the spiritual elements it has developed, as distinguished from brute force or accumulated capital.

This is the point of view from which he says:

> will effuse Egotism, and show it underlying all—and I will be the bard of personality.

Through a want of sympathy and intelligence, people have long time sneered or cavilled at this proclamation of egotism. We must strive to comprehend that Whitman does not thereby mean selfishness.

In one of his sublimest flights of the imagination Whitman describes the evolution of man out of primordial elements. He has absorbed the results of modern scientific speculation regarding planetary development and the gradual emergence of life through its successive stages on our globe. The picture is dashed in with broad touches from "the huge first Nothing" to the emergence of a conscious human soul.

> I am an acme of things accomplished, and I am an encloser of things to be.
>
> Afar down I see the huge first Nothing—I know I was even there;
> I waited unseen and always, and slept through the lethargic mist,
> And took my time, and took no harm from the fetid carbon.
>
> Long I was hugged close—long and long.
>
> Immense have been the preparations for me,
> Faithful and friendly the arms that have helped me.
>
> Cycles ferried my cradle, rowing and rowing like cheerful boatmen;
> For room to me stars kept aside in their own rings;
> They sent influences to look after what was to hold me.
>
> Before I was born out of my mother, generations guided me
> My embryo has never been torpid—nothing could overlay it.
>
> For it the nebula cohered to an orb,

The long, low strata piled to rest it on,
Vast vegetables give it sustenance,
Monstrous sauroids transported it in their mouths, and deposited it with care.

All forces have been steadily employed to complete and delight me;
Now on this spot I stand with my robust soul.

This passage will serve as a transition from the theme of cosmic enthusiasm to what Whitman considered the main motive of his prophecy. A man's self, his personality, being an indestructible integer of the universe, it follows that each one of us contains within himself sympathies with nature and sensibilities that link him to the world he lives in.

I do not doubt but the majesty and beauty of the world are latent in any iota of the world;
I do not doubt I am limitless, and that the universes are limitless—in vain I try to think how limitless.

So then, the method of self-effectuation, the training and perfecting of personality, consists in the effort to "tally nature," as Walt somewhat quaintly phrases it. The true man is one :

Who includes diversity, and is Nature,
Who is the amplitude of the earth, and the coarseness and sexuality of the earth, and the great charity of the earth, and the equilibrium also,
Who has not looked forth from the windows, the eyes for nothing, or whose brain held audiences with messengers for nothing;

Who, out of the theory of the earth, and of his or her body, understands by subtle analogies all other theories,
The theory of a city, a poem, and of the large politics of These States.

This is the new meaning given to that much-belauded and disparaged Greek phrase ζῆν κατὰ φύσιν, to live according to Nature. Whitman applies it in a very particular sense :

Now I see the secret of the making of the best persons,
It is to grow in the open air, and to eat and sleep with the earth.

You must test all the products of the human mind by comparison with things in the world around you, see how far they agree with what you find in nature, whether they are applicable to the " broadcast doings of the night and day " :

Now I re-examine philosophies and religions,

They may prove well in lecture-rooms, and yet not prove at all under the spacious clouds, and along the landscape and flowing currents.
Here is realisation;
Here is a man tallied—he realises here what he has in him;
The animals, the past, the future, light, space, majesty, love, if they are vacant of you, you are vacant of them.

He who has imbued himself with nature, and is at harmony with the world, is the proper judge, and critic, and sayer of words. To the would-be poet Whitman cries:

Can your performance face the open fields and the seaside?
Will it absorb into me as I absorb food, air—to appear again in my strength, gait, face?

To the student of his own works he says:

If you would understand me, go to the heights or water-shore;
The nearest gnat is an explanation, and a drop or motion of waves a key;
The maul, the oar, the hand-saw, second my words.

No shuttered room or school can commune with me,
But roughs and little children know me better than they.
The young mechanic is closest to me—he knows me well.

The real poems, the real words, are not what people say, but things in the world, actualities, emotions, whereof words are but the shadows and grey phantoms :

> Human bodies are words, myriads of words ;
> Air, soil, water, fire—these are words ;
> The workmanship of souls is by the inaudible words of the earth ;
> I swear there is no greatness or power that does not emulate those of the earth.
>
> Logic and sermons never convince :
> The damp of the night drives deeper into my soul ;
> The real poems (what we call poems being merely pictures),
> The poems of the privacy of the night, and of men like me.

Practising what he preaches, Whitman avers that he never composed except in the open air, and says of his own poems :

> I have read these leaves to myself in the open air—I have tried them by trees, stars, rivers.

In the prelude to one of his solemn diatribes upon the cosmic unity which connects and enfolds all creatures and all things, he represents himself alone at night beside the sea, beneath the stars, and then :

> I think a thought of the clef of the universes, and of the future.

This conception of the intimate relation which exists between human personality and the external world, penetrates the whole of Whitman's work. To cull further instances would be superfluous. But, in order to understand it and to appreciate its application, three pieces ought to be attentively studied. These are: "The Song of the Open Road," "To Working-Men," "To the Sayers of Words."

The great facts, then, are the universe and personality. The world and man. Each self alone, and for itself the measure of the world; trained and taught by nature more than by churches and traditions; by experience of life, by conduct and emotion, more than by creeds and formulas. Whitman insists upon the independence and the arrogance of self, what the Greeks called αὐτάρκεια, what the Germans call Selbst-ständigkeit. He will even sacrifice some points of conduct and morality for this spinal quality of self-reliance. Revolt against opinion, rebellion against law, indulgence in untamed proclivities, are even justified in certain cases.

I am not the poet of goodness only—I do not decline to be
 the poet of wickedness also.
What blurt is this about virtue and about vice?
Evil propels me, and reform of evil propels me—I stand
 indifferent;
My gait is no fault-finder's or rejecter's gait;
I moisten the root of all that has grown.

To enforce his doctrine of personality, Whitman insists that everything which is, exists for the individual. All doctrines, politics, civilisations, poems, arts, music, are for him. Religions have grown like leaves of grass from the individual soul. Without you, without me, without human personalities, where would all these things be?*

Whoever you are! motion and reflection are especially for
 you.
The divine ship sails the divine sea for you.

Whoever you are! you are he or she for whom the earth is
 solid and liquid,
You are he or she for whom the sun or moon hang in
 the sky,

---

* In conversation with Mr. J. W. Wallace, Whitman declared that his object in writing and publishing "Leaves of Grass" was "to arouse that something in the reader we call character . . . . not to describe things outside you—creeds, or bibles, or anything else—but arouse that which is in *you*. It *is* in you."

> For none more than you are the present and the past,
> For none more than you is immortality.
> Each man to himself, and each woman to herself, such is the word of the past and present, and the word of immortality;
> No one can acquire for another—not one!
> Not one can grow for another—not one!

In like manner, it is only through ourselves, by what each one is and has become, that we enjoy or suffer, enter into our natural heritage or are defrauded of our birthright. Consider, then, of what vast importance it is for all of us to maintain our personality in health and vigour, to abstain from habits that warp or degrade, to encourage the nobler and sweeter elements of our nature. Though Whitman proclaims himself the "poet of wickedness," he is well aware that wrong conduct, perversity, meanness, uncleanliness, are deleterious to self. "The murder is to the murderer, and comes back most to him; the theft is to the thief, the love is to the lover, the gift is to the giver, and comes back most to him; it cannot fail." Whatsoever a man soweth, that shall he also reap. The doer must suffer for his deed. There is no act that has not everlasting consequences to the agent. Each soul drees the doom of its own action and emotion. We find no immorality in Whitman's gospel of egotism.

> Charity and personal force are the only investments worth anything.
> No specification is necessary—all that a male or female does that is vigorous, benevolent, clean, is so much profit to him or her, in the unshakable order of the universe, and through the whole scope of it for ever.
>
> The young man who composedly perilled his life and lost it, has done exceedingly well for himself, without doubt.
> He who never perilled his life, but retains it to old age in riches and ease, has probably achieved nothing for himself worth mentioning.

Terrible is the doom of those who, by neglecting their health of body and soul, by shutting up their minds to natural influences, by truckling to superstitions and serving false gods, injure their own self. They have lost the greatest joy of living:

> O the joy of a manly self-hood!
> Personality—to be servile to none—to defer to none—not to any tyrant, known or unknown,
> To walk with erect carriage, a step springy and elastic,
> To look with calm gaze, or with flashing eye,
> To speak with a full sonorous voice, out of a broad chest,

> To confront with your personality all the other personalities
> of the earth.

That supremest of joys will be missed by those who do not respect self as their sole and indefeasible possession.

But what meaning does Whitman attach to this word Personality ? How does he envisage that phenomenon of self, which is the one thing certain for each separate individual who thinks and feels, and which he has therefore selected as the main motive of his prophecy ?

Personality presents itself to him, as to average man or woman, under the double aspect of soul and body, and furthermore as differentiated by sex. He appears to have believed that in this life the soul is inextricably connected with the body, so that whatever is done in the body redounds to the advantage or disadvantage of the soul. At the same time the fleshly body is destined to dissolution. It is pronounced to be " excrementitious," whereas the principle of selfhood is indestructible, and the soul may be transformed, but can never perish.

During this life, at any rate, the body constitutes a man and forms the channel of communication between his soul and outer things.*

> I too had received identity by my Body:
> That I was, I knew was of my body—and what I should be, I knew should be of my body.

The body has therefore a mystic value for Whitman, not merely because of its exceeding beauty and delightfulness, but also because it is verily the temple of the divinest of all things we know, the human soul.

> If I worship one thing more than another, it shall be the spread of my own body, or any part of it.
>
> If anything is sacred, the human body is sacred,
> And the glory and sweet of a man, is the token of manhood untainted;
> And in man or woman, a clean, strong, firm-fibred body, is beautiful as the most beautiful face.

The paramount importance of pure and wholesome manhood or womanhood becomes apparent when we reflect that:

> All comes by the body—only health puts you rapport with the universe.

---

* In conversation with Mr. J. W. Wallace at Camden, in the year 1891, Whitman spoke of "My favourite theory of physiological development underlying all."

Again, though the actual form of flesh which clothes us in this life be excrementitious, still the body in some higher sense is not doomed to die.

Of your real body, and any man's or woman's real body,
Item for item, it will elude the hands of the corpse-cleaners,
    and pass to fitting spheres,
Carrying what has accrued to it from the moment of birth to
    the moment of death.
Behold! the body includes and is the meaning, the main
    concern—and includes and is the soul;
Whoever you are! how superior and how divine is your
    body, or any part of it.

Think of the soul;
I swear to you that body of yours gives proportions to your
    soul somehow to live in other spheres;
I do not know how, but I know it is so.

No wonder, then, if Whitman, feeling thus, exclaims at times that the distinction between soul and body, so far as the individual is concerned, vanishes away.

I have said that the soul is not more than the body,
And I have said that the body is not more than the soul;
And nothing, not God, is greater to one than one's self is.

We may now ask what is Whitman's ideal of human personality. Where does he find the best type of self, the manliest man, the most womanly woman? The answer to this question is not far to seek, when we bear in mind what we already know about his preference for open life and nature. His hero is sure to be some "nonchalant and natural person"; not a man of culture or a bookworm, but one who has been born with a fine physique, capable of subduing the external world to his own purpose, and delighting in his labour; a man of healthy instincts and strong passions, vividly enjoying the boon pleasures of life, and keenly responding to the beauty and the wonder of the world.

The boy I love, the same becomes a man, not through derived power, but in his own right,

Wicked, rather than virtuous out of conformity or fear,

Fond of his sweetheart, relishing well his steak,

Unrequited love, or a slight, cutting him worse than sharp steel cuts,

First-rate to ride, to fight, to hit the bull's-eye, to sail a skiff, to sing a song, to play on the banjo,

Preferring scars, and the beard, and faces pitted with small-pox, over all latherers,

And those well tanned to those that keep out of the sun.*

* This is rather like a fragment which I have translated from the works of the little known German writer, Karl Heinrich Ulrichs:

Dearer to me is the lad village-born with sinewy members
Than the pale face of a fine town-bred effeminate youngling;

This theme is repeated with endless variations. The ground-thought recurs over and over again, and will, in the sequel, be found to dominate all his theory of the state politic.

Myself and mine gymnastic ever,
To stand the cold or heat—to take good aim with a gun—to sail a boat—to manage horses—to beget superb children,
To speak readily and clearly—to feel at home among common people,
And to hold our own in terrible positions, on land and sea.

Not for an embroiderer;
(There will always be plenty of embroiderers—I welcome them also;)
But for the fibre of things, and for inherent men and women.

Not to chisel ornaments,
But to chisel with free strokes the heads and limbs of plenteous supreme Gods, that these States may realise them, walking and talking.

Such men Whitman calls "athletes," and the women he demands for the back-bone of a nation

Dearer to me is a groom, a tamer of horses, a hunter,
Yea, or a sailor on board: but dear to me down to the heart's depth,
Dearest of all are the young, steel-thewed, magnificent soldiers—
Be it the massive form of a black-browed insolent guardsman,
Or a blue-eyed hussar with the down new-fledged on his firm lip—
Who with clanking spurs and martial tread when they meet me,
Know not how goodly they are, the sight of them how overwhelming.

must equally be "athletic." He is convinced that in such personalities the soul reaches its maximum of magnetic attraction and persuasiveness.

Here rises the fluid and attaching character;
The fluid and attaching character is the freshness and sweetness of man and woman;

Toward the fluid and attaching character exudes the sweat of the love of young and old;
From it falls distilled the charm that mocks beauty and attainments;
Toward it heaves the shuddering longing ache of contact.

I and mine do not convince by arguments, similes, rhymes;
We convince by our presence.

"To effuse magnetism," to attract and persuade by merely being vigorous and sound and free, is the crown and glory of a perfected personality.

Do you not see how it would serve to have such a body and soul, that when you enter the crowd, an atmosphere of desire and command enters with you, and every one is impressed with your personality?

Those severe and awful utterances, "A Hand-Mirror," "To a President," "Of Persons Arrived at High Positions," and some pregnant passages from "A Leaf of Faces," point the opposite lesson: how useless it is to have conquered wealth, place, honours, if one has lost his own soul, corrupted his own live body, neglected and dishonoured his own self.

IV

THE transition from Personality to Sex offers no difficulty. Sex, the passions, the affections, love, are clearly the main things in life.

In his treatment of Love, Whitman distinguishes two broad kinds of human affection; the one being the ordinary sexual relation, the other comradeship or an impassioned relation between man and man. The former he describes as "amativeness," the latter as "adhesiveness." There is no reason why both forms of emotion should not co-exist in the same person. Indeed Whitman makes it plain that a completely endowed individuality, one who, as Horace might have said, is "entirely rounded and without ragged edges," will be highly susceptible of both. The exact bearing of amativeness and adhesiveness upon one another, and upon the spiritual nature of the individual, has been fully expressed in the following poem:

Fast-anchored eternal O love ! O woman I love !
O bride ! O wife ! more resistless than I can tell, the thought of you !
Then separate, as disembodied or another born,
Ethereal, the last athletic reality, my consolation,
I ascend, I float in the regions of your love, O man,
O sharer of my roving life.

Since this is the most condensed and weighty of Whitman's utterances upon the subject of love, every word in it may be supposed to have been carefully considered. It is not therefore insignificant to notice that, in the edition of 1860-61, "primeval" stood for "fast-anchored" in the first line, and "the purest born" for "or another born" in the third line.

The section of his complete works which deals exclusively with sexual love, is entitled "Children of Adam." The frankness and the rankness of the pieces composing this chapter called down a storm of insults, calumnies, unpopularity, on Whitman. Yet the attitude which he assumed as poet and prophet demanded this frankness, while the spirit of his treatment deprived the subject-matter of its rankness.

His originality consisted, I have said, in giving the idealism of poetry and powerful emotion to the blank results of modern science. Now it is in the very nature of science to consider nothing as "common or unclean," to accept all the facts presented to its vision with indifference, caring for nothing in the process of analysis except the proof of reality, the elucidation of truth. Science, in her wise impartiality, regards morbid phenomena, disease and decay, crime and aberration, as worthy of attention, upon the same lines as healthy and normal products. She knows that pathology is an indispensable adjunct to the study of organic structure.

Sharing the scientific spirit in his quality of poet, Whitman was not called to celebrate what is unhealthy and abnormal in humanity. That is a proper subject for the laboratory. The poet's function is to stimulate and to invigorate. It is his duty to insist upon what is wholesome, the things in life which conduce to organic growth, the natural instincts and normal appetites upon which the continuation of the species, the energy of the individual, the welfare of the family, the fabric of the commonwealth, eventually rest. Feeling thus, and being penetrated with the scientific spirit,

Whitman was justified in claiming the whole of healthy manhood and womanhood for his province. To exclude sex from his account of human nature would have been absurd; for it is precisely sex by which men and women are differentiated; sex which brings them into mutual relations of amativeness; sex which determines the preservation and the future of the species. The inspiration which prompted him, first among modern poets, to penetrate the blank results of science with imagination and emotion, led him inevitably to a frank treatment of sexual relations. Each portion of the healthy human body had for a thinker of his type to be considered "sweet and clean." He could not shrink from the facts of paternity and maternity, these being the most important both for men and women, and through them for society at large. For him "the parts and poems of the body" are not "of the body only, but of the soul"—indeed "these are the soul." Following the impulse which forced him to insist upon a vigorous and healthy personality or self as the fundamental integer of human life, he proceeded to impress upon his nation the paramount duty of maintaining a robust and healthy breed. Scientific pathology may be left to deal with abnormalities and diseases. The social conscience is sufficiently, if dimly, acquainted with those evils. For the poet, who has accepted the scientific point of view, it is enough to indicate their wrongness. But he enjoys the privilege of proclaiming the beauty and the goodness of functions and organs which constitute the central reality of human life. To recognise the dignity of sex, to teach personalities, both male and female, that they have the right to take a pride in it, and that this pride is their duty, was for a poet of Whitman's stamp a prime consideration. Those mediæval lies regarding sexual sinfulness, those foolish panegyrics of chaste abstinence, those base insinuations of foul-minded priests, had to be swept away— not by polemic or vituperation, but by a plain proclamation of the truth which had been veiled from sight so long. Delicacy in matters of sex had become indelicacy by a false habit of envisaging the fact. All falsehood is inconsistent with science and injurious to the best interests of society.

Having entered upon this region with the objects I have hinted at—a recognition of fundamental truths, an acceptance of scientific as opposed to theological principles, a deep sense of personality, and a conviction that the maintenance of the breed at its highest level of efficiency is a prime condition of national well-being— Whitman naturally treated the ordinary sexual relations with a breadth and simplicity which appear to more sophisticated minds as brutal. He does not shrink from images and descriptions, from metaphors and phrases, as closely borrowed from the facts of sex as are his pictures of the outer world, or his transcripts from the occupations of mankind. Sex, being for him so serious and excellent a thing, has the right to equal freedom of speech with sunrise or sunsetting, the stars in their courses, the woods and fields, the industries of carpenter or typesetter, the courage of soldiers, the inevitable fact of death. Therefore he speaks plainly about many things which hitherto were tacitly ignored in poetry, or were touched upon by seekers after obscene literary effects. It is not inconsequent that he should have been accused of indecency, because the things he talked of had so long been held to be indecent. Wishing to remove the stigma of indecency and obscenity, which he rightly considered due to conventionally imported prejudices, he had to face the misconstruction of those who could not comprehend his real intention.

Whitman thought and wrote habitually, not with people of culture, refined tastes, literary and social traditions in view, but for the needs and aspirations of what he called "the divine average." He aimed at depicting robust and sane humanity in his verse. He wanted to brace character, and to create through his art-work a type applicable to all sorts and conditions of men, irrespective of their previous differentiation by specific temperament or class-association. For this reason, his treatment of the sexual relations will be felt by some persons not only to be crudely frank in detail, but also to lack delicacy in its general outlines. The overwhelming attractions of sex, swaying the physique of men and women, are broadly insisted upon. The intercourse established in matrimony is regarded not so much as an intellectual and moral union, but as an association for mutual assistance in the labours of life, and for the production of noble human specimens. It is an Adamic hygienic view of marriage, satisfying the instincts of the primeval man. Take this passage, in which he describes the qualities of the help-mate for his typical male.

Without shame the man I like knows and avows the deliciousness of his sex,
Without shame the woman I like knows and avows hers.

Now I will dismiss myself from impassive women,
I will go stay with her who waits for me, and with those women that are warm-blooded and sufficient for me ;
I see that they understand me, and do not deny me :
I see that they are worthy of me—I will be the robust husband of these women.

They are not one jot less than I am,
They are tanned in the face by shining suns and blowing winds,
Their flesh has the old divine suppleness and strength,
They know how to swim, row, ride, wrestle, shoot, run, strike, retreat, advance, resist, defend themselves,
They are ultimate in their own right—they are calm, clear, well-possessed of themselves.

I draw you close to me, you women !
I cannot let you go, I would do you good,
I am for you, and you are for me, not only for our own sake, but for others' sake ;

Envelop'd in you sleep greater heroes and bards,
They refuse to awake at the touch of any man but me.

It is obvious, from this slightly humorous, but pregnant, passage, that Whitman abandoned those dregs of mediæval sentimentalism and platonism, which filtering through the middle-class minds of an unchivalrous modern age, have resulted in commonplace notions about "the weaker and the fairer sex," "woman's mission to console and elevate," the "protection rendered by the stronger to the frailer," "the feminine ornament of our homes"—notions and phrases which the active-minded and able-bodied woman of the present day repudiates, and from the thraldom of which she is rapidly working out her way toward freedom. Whitman, to use a phrase of Clough, looked upon love as "fellow-service." He recognised the woman's right to share alike with man in labour and in privilege. And it was not for nothing, as appears from some sentences in the quotation, that he spoke in another place about "the athletic American matron." *

---

* In the preface to the 1872 edition of "Leaves of Grass," Whitman asserts that this book "is, in its intentions, the song of a great composite *democratic individual*, male or female."

A theory of sexual relations, so primitive, so archetypal, so based and planted on the primal needs and instincts, must of necessity lack much of delicacy and fine gradations. It is, however, bracing to return to this from the psychological studies of the modern French school, from such silly and nauseous lucubrations as Bourget's "Physiologie de l'Amour Moderne," from all that stifling literature of "L'Amour Coupable," which lands us at last in nothing better than what Whitman calls "the sly settee, and the unwholesome adulterous couple."

There is an Æschylean largeness, a Lucretian energy, in Whitman's "Children of Adam." Sex is once again recognised; not in its aspect of the boudoir, the alcove, the brothel; but as the bass-note of the world, the universal Pan, unseen, yet omnipresent, felt by all, responded to by all, without which the whole vast symphony of things would have for man no value. By subtle associations, he connects the life of nature, in dewy forests and night-winds, in scents of fruits and pungent plants, in crushed herbs, and the rustling of rain-drenched foliage against our faces, with impressions of the sexual imagination. He finds the choicest images to shadow forth the acts of sex.

> The hairy wild bee that murmurs and hankers up and down —that gripes the full-grown lady-flower, curves upon her with amorous firm legs, takes his will of her, and holds himself tremulous and tight till he is satisfied.

That is audacious, in spite of its consummate style, a critic will exclaim. But the same critic, being accustomed by habit to the exercise, reads with equanimity the long-drawn paragraphs and chapters which lay bare the latest secrets of the "sly settee." The boudoir, the alcove, the brothel, have come to be recognised as legitimate subjects for analytical art. Even Bourget, even Catulle Mendès, are accepted and acclaimed. From these taints of the city and civilisation Whitman calls us away. He says in passing:

> Have you seen the fool that corrupted his own live body? or the fool that corrupted her own live body?
> For they do not conceal themselves, and cannot conceal themselves.

Here and there he returns to this point and repeats the warning. He insists upon the truth that sins against the body, self-contamination, uncleanly lusts and refinements of sensuality, carry their own punishment. But he knows that their analysis in literature, except for the professed pathologist and psychiatrist, is harmful to the manhood of a nation; whereas the rehabitation of healthy and legitimate functions restores the natural man to a sense of his own dignity and responsibility. Nor does Whitman neglect that superflux of sense, which also claims a part in human life, that phallic ecstasy of which the pagan poets sang. A much-criticised piece from " Children of Adam " puts the matter very plainly. It is called " Native Moments," and need not be enlarged upon. Were we not expressly told by him that it is useless to extract a coherent system from his utterances, we might be puzzled to explain the logical connection of that poem with the rest of the section. I take it that he recognised the right and the necessity of " native moments " in that free play of the normal senses which he is upholding. Only, the ground-thoughts which penetrate the whole of his work upon this topic, the pervading essence whereof will remain longest with those who have imbibed its spirit, are expressed in lines like these :

If any thing is sacred, the human body is sacred,
And the glory and sweet of a man is the token of manhood untainted ;
And in man or woman, a clean, strong, firm-fibred body is beautiful as the most beautiful face.

If Æschylus could come again, he would recognise Whitman's treatment of Aphrodite as akin to these lines of his own :

> Love throbs in holy heaven to wound the earth ;
> And love still prompts the land to yearn for bridals;
> The rain that falls in rivers from the sky,
> Impregnates earth, and she brings forth for men
> The flocks and herds and life of teeming Ceres;
> The bloom of forests by dews hymeneal
> Is perfected : in all which things I rule.

If we are to have sex handled openly in literature—and I do not see why we should not have it, or how we are to avoid it—surely it is better to be in the company of poets like Æschylus and Whitman, who place human love among the large and universal mysteries of nature, than to dwell with theologians who confound its simple truth with sinfulness, or with self-dubbed "psychologues" who dabble in its morbid pruriencies.

V

THE section of Whitman's works which deals with adhesiveness, or the love of comrades, is fully as important, and in some ways more difficult to deal with, than his "Children of Adam." He gave it the title "Calamus," from the root of a water-rush, adopted by him as the symbol of this love.* Here the element of spirituality in passion, of romantic feeling, and of deep enduring sentiment, which was almost conspicuous by its absence from the section on sexual love, emerges into vivid prominence, and lends peculiar warmth of poetry to the artistic treatment. We had to expect so much from the poem quoted by me at the commencement of this disquisition. There Whitman described the love of man for woman as "fast-anchor'd, eternal"; the thought of the bride, the wife, as

* Its botanical name is Acorus Calamus. We call it "sweet-rush" or "sweet sedge."

"more resistless than I can tell." But for the love of man for man he finds quite a different class of descriptive phrases : " separate, disembodied, another born, ethereal, the last athletic reality, my consolation." He hints that we have left the realm of sex and sense, and have ascended into a different and rarer atmosphere, where passion, though it has not lost its strength, is clarified. " Largior hic æther, et campos lumine vestit purpureo."

This emphatic treatment of an emotion which is usually talked about under the vague and formal term of friendship, gives peculiar importance to " Calamus." No man in the modern world has expressed so strong a conviction that " manly attachment," " athletic love," " the high towering love of comrades," is a main factor in human life, a virtue upon which society will have to lay its firm foundations, and a passion equal in permanence, superior in spirituality, to the sexual affection. Whitman regards this emotion not only as the " consolation " of the individual, but also as a new and hitherto unapprehended force for stimulating national vitality.

There is no softness or sweetness in his treatment of this theme. His tone is sustained throughout at a high pitch of virile enthusiasm, which, at the same time, vibrates with acutest feeling, thrills with an undercurrent of the tenderest sensibility. Not only the sublimest thoughts and aspirations, but also the shyest, most shame-faced, yearnings are reserved for this love. At one time he exclaims:

O I think it is not for life that I am chanting here my chant of lovers—I think it must be for Death,
For how calm, how solemn it grows, to ascend to the atmosphere of lovers,
Death or life I am then indifferent—my soul declines to prefer,
I am not sure but the high soul of lovers welcomes death most;
Indeed, O Death, I think now these leaves mean precisely the same as you mean;
Grow up taller, sweet leaves, that I may see! Grow up out of my breast!
Spring away from the concealed heart there!
Do not fold yourselves so, in your pink-tinged roots, timid leaves!
Do not remain down there so ashamed, herbage of my breast!

The leaves are Whitman's emotions and the poems they engender; the root from which they spring is "manly attachment," "athletic love," symbolised for him in the blushing root of the pond-calamus which he plucked one day and chose to be the emblem of the love of lovers :

O here I last saw him that tenderly loves me—and returns again, never to separate from me,
And this, O this shall henceforth be the token of comrades— this Calamus-root shall,
Interchange it, youths, with each other ! Let none render it back !

At another time, in minor key, he writes as follows :

O you when I often and silently come where you are, that I may be with you;
As I walk by your side, or sit near, or remain in the same room with you,
Little you know the subtle, electric fire that for your sake is playing within me.

These extracts were necessary, because there is some misapprehension abroad regarding the precise nature of what Whitman meant by " Calamus." His method of treatment has, to a certain extent, exposed him to misconstruction. Still, as his friend and commentator, Mr. Burroughs, puts it : " The sentiment is primitive, athletic, taking form in all manner of large and homely out-of-door images, and springs, as any one may see, directly from the heart and experience of the poet." The language has a passionate glow, a warmth of devotion, beyond anything to which the world is used in the celebration of friendship. At the same time the false note of insincerity or sensuousness is never heard. The melody is in the Dorian mood—recalling to our minds that fellowship in arms which flourished among the Dorian tribes, and formed the chivalry of pre-historic Hellas.

In the preface to the 1880 edition of " Leaves of Grass" and " Two Rivulets," Whitman gives his own explanation of " Calamus," and of the feelings which inspired that section of his work.

Something more may be added—for, while I am about it, I would make a full confession. I also sent out " Leaves of Grass" to arouse and set flowing in men's and women's hearts, young and old, endless streams of living, pulsating love and friendship, directly from them to myself, now and ever. To this terrible, irrepressible yearning (surely more or less down underneath in most human souls), this never-satisfied appetite for sympathy and this boundless offering of sympathy, this universal democratic comradeship, this old, eternal, yet ever-new interchange of adhesiveness, so fitly emblematic of America, I have given in that book, undisguisedly, declaredly, the openest expression. Besides, important as they are in my purpose as emotional expressions for humanity, the special meaning of the "Calamus," cluster of "Leaves of Grass" (and more or less running through the book and cropping out in "Drum Taps"), mainly resides in its political significance. In my opinion, it is by a fervent accepted development of comradeship, the beautiful and sane affection of man for man, latent in all the young fellows, north and south, east and west—it is by this, I say, and by what goes directly and indirectly along with it, that the United States of the future (I cannot too often repeat) are to be the most effectually welded together, intercalated, annealed into a living union.

This being so, Whitman never suggests that comradeship may occasion the development of physical desire. On the other hand, he does not in set terms condemn desires, or warn his disciples against their perils. There is indeed a distinctly sensuous side to his conception of adhesiveness. To a Western Boy he says:

If you be not silently selected by lovers, and do not silently select lovers,
Of what use is it that you seek to become elect of mine?

Like Plato, in the *Phædrus*, Whitman describes an enthusiastic type of masculine emotion, leaving its private details to the moral sense and special inclination of the individuals concerned.

A STUDY OF WALT WHITMAN

The poet himself appears to be not wholly unconscious that there are dangers and difficulties involved in the highly-pitched emotions he is praising. The whole tenor of two carefully-toned compositions, entitled " Whoever you are, Holding me now in hand," and " Trickle, Drops," suggest an underlying sense of spiritual conflict. The following poem, again, is sufficiently significant and typical to call for literal transcription :

Earth, my likeness !
Though you look so impassive, ample and spheric there,
I now suspect that is not all ;
I now suspect there is something fierce in you, eligible to burst forth ;
For an athlete is enamoured of me—and I of him,
But toward him there is something fierce and terrible in me, eligible to burst forth,
I dare not tell it in word—not even in these songs.

The reality of Whitman's feeling, the intense delight which he derives from the personal presence and physical contact of a beloved man, find luminous expression in " A Glimpse," "Recorders ages hence," "When I heard at the Close of Day," " I saw in Louisiana a Live-Oak growing," " Long I thought that Knowledge alone would suffice me,"* "O Tan-faced Prairie-Boy," and "Vigil Strange I kept on the Field one Night."†

It is clear then that, in his treatment of comradeship, or the impassioned love of man for man, Whitman has struck a keynote, to the emotional intensity of which the modern world is unaccustomed. It therefore becomes of much importance to discover the poet-prophet's *Stimmung*—his radical instinct with regard to the moral quality of the feeling he encourages. Studying his works by their own light, and by the light of their author's character, interpreting each part by reference to the whole and in the spirit of the whole, an impartial critic will, I think, be drawn to the conclusion that what he calls the "adhesiveness" of comradeship is meant to have no interblending with the "amativeness" of sexual love. Personally, it is undeniable that Whitman possessed a specially keen sense of the fine restraint and continence, the cleanliness and chastity, that are inseparable

---

* Not included in the "Complete Poems and Prose." It will be found in "Leaves of Grass," Boston, 1860-61.

† The two last are from "Drum-Taps."

from the perfectly virile and physically complete nature of healthy manhood. Still we have the right to predicate the same ground-qualities in the early Dorians, those founders of the martial institution of Greek love ; and yet it is notorious to students of Greek civilisation that the lofty sentiment of their masculine chivalry was intertwined with much that is repulsive to modern sentiment.

Whitman does not appear to have taken some of the phenomena of contemporary morals into due account, although he must have been aware of them. Else he would have foreseen that, human nature being what it is, we cannot expect to eliminate all sensual alloy from emotions raised to a high pitch of passionate intensity, and that permanent elements within the midst of our society will imperil the absolute purity of the ideal he attempts to establish. It is obvious that those unenviable mortals who are the inheritors of sexual anomalies, will recognise their own emotion in Whitman's " superb friendship, exalté, previously unknown," which " waits, and has been always waiting, latent in all men," the " something fierce in me, eligible to burst forth," "ethereal comradeship," "the last athletic reality." Had I not the strongest proof in Whitman's private correspondence with myself that he repudiated any such deductions from his "Calamus," I admit that I should have regarded them as justified; and I am not certain whether his own feelings upon this delicate topic may not have altered since the time when "Calamus" was first composed.

These considerations do not, however, affect the spiritual quality of his ideal. After acknowledging, what Whitman omitted to perceive, that there are inevitable points of contact between sexual anomaly and his doctrine of comradeship, the question now remains whether he has not suggested the way whereby abnormal instincts may be moralised and raised to higher value. In other words, are those exceptional instincts provided in "Calamus" with the means of their salvation from the filth and mire of brutal appetite? It is difficult to answer this question; for the issue involved is nothing less momentous than the possibility of evoking a new chivalrous enthusiasm, analogous to that of primitive Hellenic society, from emotions which are at present classified among the turpitudes of human nature.

Let us look a little closer at the expression which Whitman has given to his own feelings about friendship. The first thing that strikes us is the mystic emblem he has chosen for masculine love. That is the water-plant, or scented rush, called "Calamus," which springs in wild places, "in paths untrodden, in the growth by margins of pond-waters." He has chosen these "emblematic and capricious blades" because of their shyness, their aromatic perfume, their aloofness from the patent life of the world. He calls them "sweet leaves, pink-tinged roots, timid leaves," "scented herbage of my breast." Finally, he says :*

Here my last words, and the most baffling,
Here the frailest leaves of me, and yet my strongest-lasting.
Here I shade down, and hide my thoughts—I do not expose them,
And yet they expose me more than all my other poems.

The manliness of the emotion which is thus

---

* This I cannot find in "Complete Poems and Prose." It is included in the Boston edition, 1860-61, and the Camden edition, 1876.

so shyly, allegorically indicated, appears in the magnificent address to soldiers at the close of the great war: " Over the Carnage rose Prophetic a Voice."* Its tenderness emerges in the elegy on a slain comrade :†

Vigil for boy of responding kisses (never again on earth responding):
Vigil for comrade swiftly slain—vigil I never forget, how as day brightened,
I rose from the chill ground, and folded my soldier well in his blanket,
And buried him where he fell.

Its pathos and clinging intensity transpire through the last lines of the following piece, which may have been suggested by the legends of David and Jonathan, Achilles and Patroclus, Orestes and Pylades :‡

* "Drum Taps." Complete Poems, p. 247.
† *Ibid.* p. 238.
‡ "Leaves of Grass." Complete Poems, p. 107. Since writing the above, I have been privileged to read a series of letters addressed by Whitman to a young man, whom I will call P., and who was tenderly beloved by him. They throw a flood of life upon " Calamus," and are superior to any commentary. It is greatly to be hoped that they may be published. Whitman, it seems, met P. at Washington not long before the year 1869, when the lad was about eighteen years of age. They soon became attached, Whitman's friendship being returned with at least equal warmth by P. The letters breathe a purity and simplicity of affection, a *naïveté* and reasonableness, which are very

When I peruse the conquered fame of heroes, and the victories
  of mighty generals,
I do not envy the generals,
Nor the President in his Presidency, nor the rich in his great
  house;
But when I read of the brotherhood of lovers, how it was with
  them,
How through life, through dangers, odium, unchanging, long
  and long,
Through youth, and through middle and old age, how un-
  faltering, how affectionate and faithful they were,
Then I am pensive—I hastily put down the book, and walk
  away, filled with the bitterest envy.

But Whitman does not conceive of comradeship as a merely personal possession, delightful to the friends it links in bonds of amity. He regards it eventually as a social and political virtue. This human emotion is destined to cement society and to render commonwealths inviolable. Reading

remarkable considering the unmistakable intensity of the emotion. Throughout them, Whitman shows the tenderest and wisest care for his young friend's welfare, helps him in material ways, and bestows upon him the best advice, the heartiest encouragement, without betraying any sign of patronage or preaching. Illness soon attacked Walt. He retired to Camden, and P., who was employed as "baggage-master on the freight-trains" of a railway, was for long unable to visit him. There is something very wistful in the words addressed from a distance by the aging poet to this "son of responding kisses." I regret that we do not possess P.'s answers. Yet, probably, to most readers, they would not appear highly interesting; for it is clear he was only an artless and uncultured workman.

some of his poems, we are carried back to ancient Greece—to Plato's *Symposium*, to Philip gazing on the sacred band of Thebans after the fight at Chaeronea.*

I dream'd in a dream, I saw a city invincible to the attacks of the whole of the rest of the earth;
I dream'd that was the new City of Friends;
Nothing was greater there than the quality of robust love—it led the rest;
It was seen every hour in the actions of the men of that city,
And in all their looks and words.

And again : †

I believe the main purport of These States is to found a superb friendship, exalté, previously unknown,
Because I perceive it waits, and has been always waiting, latent in all men.

And once again : ‡

Come, I will make the continent indissoluble;
I will make the most splendid race the sun ever yet shone upon;
I will make divine magnetic lands,
    With the love of comrades,
        With the life-long love of comrades.

---

* Complete Poems, p. 109. Compare, " I hear it was charged against me," *ibid.* p. 107.

† Complete Poems, p. 110.

‡ Camden edition, 1876, p. 127. Complete Poems, p. 99. Compare " Democratic Vistas," Complete Prose, p. 247, note.

> I will plant companionship thick as trees all along the rivers
>   of America, and along the shores of the great lakes, and
>   all over the prairies;
> I will make inseparable cities, with their arms about each
>   other's necks;
>   By the love of comrades,
>   By the manly love of comrades.
>
> For you these from me, O Democracy, to serve you *ma femme!*
> For you, for you I am trilling these songs.

We may return from this analysis to the inquiry whether anything like a new chivalry is to be expected from the doctrines of "Calamus," which shall in the future utilise for noble purposes some of those unhappy instincts which at present run to waste in vice and shame. It may be asked what these passions have in common with the topic of Whitman's prophecy? They have this in common with it. Whitman recognises among the sacred emotions and social virtues, destined to regenerate political life and to cement nations, an intense, jealous, throbbing, sensitive, expectant love of man for man: a love which yearns in absence, droops under the sense of neglect, revives at the return of the beloved: a love that finds honest delight in hand-touch, meeting lips, hours of privacy, close personal contact. He proclaims this love to be not only a daily fact in the present, but also a saving and ennobling aspiration. While he expressly repudiates, disowns, and brands as "damnable" all "morbid inferences" which may be drawn by malevolence or vicious cunning from his doctrine, he is prepared to extend the gospel of comradeship to the whole human race. He expects democracy, the new social and political medium, the new religious ideal of mankind, to develop and extend "that fervid comradeship," and by its means to counterbalance and to spiritualise what is vulgar and materialistic in the modern world. "Democracy," he maintains, "infers such loving comradeship, as its most inevitable twin or counterpart, without which it will be incomplete, in vain, and incapable of perpetuating itself."*

If this be not a dream, if he is right in believing that "threads of manly friendship, fond and loving, pure and sweet, strong and life-long, carried to degrees hitherto unknown," will pene-

---

* These prose passages are taken from "Democratic Vistas," cited above, p. 94, note.

trate the organism of society, " not only giving tone to individual character, and making it unprecedentedly emotional, muscular, heroic, and refined, but having deepest relations to general politics"—then are we perhaps justified in foreseeing here the advent of an enthusiasm which shall rehabilitate those outcast instincts, by giving them a spiritual atmosphere, an environment of recognised and healthy emotions, wherein to expand at liberty and purge away the grossness and the madness of their pariahdom?

This prospect, like all ideals, until they are realised in experience, may seem fantastically visionary. Moreover, the substance of human nature is so mixed that it would perhaps be fanatical to expect from Whitman's chivalry of "adhesiveness," a more immaculate purity than was attained by the mediæval chivalry of "amativeness." Nevertheless, that mediæval chivalry, the great emotional product of feudalism, though it fell short of its own aspiration, bequeathed incalculable good to modern society by refining and clarifying the crudest of male appetites. In like manner, this democratic chivalry, announced by Whitman, may be destined to absorb, control, and elevate those darker, more mysterious, apparently abnormal appetites, which we know to be widely diffused and ineradicable in the ground-work of human nature.

Returning from the dream, the vision of a future possibility, it will, at any rate, be conceded that Whitman has founded comradeship, the enthusiasm which binds man to man in fervent love, upon a natural basis. Eliminating classical associations of corruption, ignoring the perplexed questions of a guilty passion doomed by law and popular antipathy to failure, he begins anew with sound and primitive humanity. There he discovers "a superb friendship, exalté, previously unknown." He perceives that "it waits, and has been always waiting, latent in all men." His method of treatment, fearless, and uncowed by any thought of evil, his touch upon the matter, chaste and wholesome and aspiring, reveal the possibility of restoring in all innocence to human life a portion of its alienated or unclaimed moral birthright.

It were well to close upon this note. The half, as the Greeks said, is more than the whole; and the time has not yet come to raise the question whether the love of man for man shall be elevated through a hitherto unapprehended chivalry to nobler powers, even as the barbarous love of man for woman once was. This question at the present moment is deficient in actuality. The world cannot be invited to entertain it.

VI

THE passages which have been quoted in illustration of Whitman's views regarding man and the universe, and the paramount importance of self or personality, leaves no doubt as to how he must have treated the subject of " Democracy."

The inscription placed upon the forefront of " Leaves of Grass," contains this paragraph :

> Nor cease at the theme of One's-Self. I speak the word of the modern, the word EN-MASSE.

In another place, he says :

> My comrade!
> For you, to share with me two greatnesses—a third one, rising inclusive and more resplendent,
> The greatness of Love and Democracy—and the greatness of Religion.

Whitman's comrade, the athlete, the " nonchalant and natural," the " powerful uneducated person," whom his heart desires, enters into full enjoyment of self through love and liberty, both blending in that sublimer conception of the cosmos and our place in it, which forms the groundwork of religion.

What the word "En-Masse" means for Whitman is expressed at large throughout his writings. It corresponds to another of his chosen phrases, "the divine average," "ever the most precious in the common." An exact light is thrown upon it by the following passage:

I speak the pass-word primeval—I give the sign of Democracy;
By God! I will accept nothing which all cannot have their counterpart of on the same terms.

Thus Democracy implies the absolute equality of heritage possessed by every man and woman in the good and evil of this life. It also involves the conception that there is nothing beautiful or noble which may not be discovered in the simplest human being. As regards physical structure :*

Whoever you are! how superb and how divine is your body, or any part of it.

As regards emotions and passions which throb and pulsate in the individual : †

---

* Starting from "Paumanok," 14.   † "Walt Whitman," 33.

Wherever the human heart beats with terrible throes out of its ribs.

"Whoever" and "wherever" are the emphatic words in these quotations. The human body in itself is august; the heart has tragedy implicit in its life-beats. It does not signify *whose* body, or *whose* heart. Here, there, and everywhere, the seeing eye finds majesty, the sentient intelligence detects the stuff of drama.

The same principle is applied to the whole sphere of Nature. Miracles need not be sought in special occurrences, in phenomena which startle us out of our ordinary way of regarding the universe : *

To me, every hour of the light and dark is a miracle,
Every inch of space is a miracle,
Every square yard of the surface of the earth is spread with the same,
Every cubic foot of the interior swarms with the same;
Every spear of grass—the frames, limbs, organs of men and women, and all that concern them,
All these to me are unspeakable miracles.

At this point science shakes hands with the democratic ideal : for science proves that the

* "Miracles.'

smallest atom, the most insignificant vibrio, the most repulsive microbe, partakes of the universal life no less than do the so-called lords of creation. We are not forced to gaze upon the starry heavens, or to shudder at islands overwhelmed by volcanic throes, in order to spy out the marvellous. Wonders are always present in the material world as in the spiritual : *

A morning-glory at my window satisfies me more than the metaphysics of books.

The heroic lies within our reach, if we but stretch a finger forth to touch it : †

Lads ahold of fire-engines and hook-and-ladder ropes no less to me than the Gods of the antique wars ;
Minding their voices peal through the crash of destruction,
Their brawny limbs passing safe over charred laths—their white foreheads whole and unhurt out of the flames.

Whitman expels miracles from the region of mysticism, only to find a deeper mysticism in the world of which he forms a part, and miracles in commonplace occurrences. He dethrones the gods of old pantheons, because he sees God everywhere around him. He discrowns the heroes of

* "Walt Whitman," 154.   † *Ibid.* 41.

myth and romance; but greets their like again among his living comrades. What is near to his side, beneath his feet, upon the trees around him, in the men and women he consorts with, bears comparison with things far off and rarities imagined : *

I believe a leaf of grass is no less than the journey-work of the stars. . . . .

And the running blackberry would adorn the parlours of heaven. . . . .

And I could come every afternoon of my life to look at the farmer's girl boiling her iron tea-kettle and baking shortcake.

It is the faculty of the seer, of one who has understood the wonder of the world, whose eyes pierce below the surface, to recognise divinity in all that lives and breathes upon our planet : †

Painters have painted their swarming groups, and the centre figure of all;

From the head of the centre figure spreading a nimbus of gold-coloured light;

But I paint myriads of heads, but paint no head without its nimbus of gold-coloured light;

From my hand, from the brain of every man and woman it streams, effulgently flowing for ever.

* "Walt Whitman," 31. † "Leaves of Grass," 4.

Pursuing this line of thought into the region of plastic art, we find the elements of dignity and beauty apparent in all shapes of sane and healthy manhood : *

The expression of the face balks accounts ;
But the expression of a well-made man appears not only in his face,
It is in his limbs and joints also, it is curiously in the joints of his hips and wrists ;
It is in his walk, the carriage of his neck, the flex of his waist and knees—dress does not hide him ;
The strong, sweet, supple quality he has, strikes through the cotton and flannel.
To see him pass conveys as much as the best poem, perhaps more ;
You linger to see his back, and the back of his neck and shoulder-side.

Minor passages from Whitman's writings might be culled in plenty, which illustrate these general principles. He is peculiarly rich in subjects indicated for the sculptor or the painter, glowing with his own religious sense of beauty inherent in the simplest folk : †

The beauty of all adventurous and daring persons,
The beauty of wood-boys and wood-men, with their clear, untrimmed faces.

* "I sing the Body Electric," 2.
† "Song of the Broad Axe," 3 ; "Walt Whitman," 33 ; *ibid.* 13.

Coming home with the silent and dark-cheeked bush-boy—
    riding behind him at the drape of the day.

  .   .   .   .   .   .

The negro holds firmly the reins of his four horses—the block
    sways underneath on its tied-over chain;
The negro that drives the dray of the stone-yard—steady and
    tall he stands, poised on one leg on the string-piece;
His blue shirt exposes his ample neck and breast, and loosens
    over his hip-band;
His glance is calm and commanding—he tosses the slouch of
    his hat away from his forehead;
The sun falls on his crispy hair and moustache—falls on the
    black of his polished and perfect limbs.

Detached from their context, the paragraphs which I have quoted suffer from apparent crudity and paradox. It is only by absorbing Whitman's poems in copious draughts, as I have elsewhere said, by submitting to his manner and sympathising with his mood, that a conception can be formed of the wealth with which he scatters plastic suggestions, and of the precision with which he notes down line and colour.

The essence of the democratic spirit, so far as Whitman helps us to understand it, has been sufficiently indicated. The divine in nature and humanity is everywhere, if we can penetrate the husk of commonplace and reach the poetry of things. There are, indeed, degrees in its manifestation. Special revelations, as in the life of Buddha or of Christ, for instance, do not rank in the same class with the "ever recurring miracle of the sunrise." The heroism of an engine-driver, performing his duty, has not exactly the same moral quality, the same complexity of spiritual forces in play together at one moment, as the self-dedication of Menoikeus for the welfare of his native city, or the oblation of their lives by Cratinus and Aristodemus in order to save Athens from a godsent plague.

The pioneer of democratic enthusiasm wishes mainly to remind the world that our eyes have too long been blinded to one cardinal truth—the truth that virtues and beauties, wherever found, are of like quality, and their essence equally divine. Whitman insists upon this truth in a passage, which sounds paradoxical, but the grotesqueness of which is calculated to arouse intelligence:[*]

[*] "Walt Whitman," 41.

Three scythes at harvest whizzing in a row from three lusty angels with shirts bagged out at their waists;
The snag-toothed hostler, with red hair, redeeming sins past and to come,
Selling all he possesses, travelling on foot to fee lawyers for his brother, and sit by him while he is tried for forgery.

The resplendent manhood of Michael, Gabriel, Raphael, "starred from Jehovah's gorgeous armoury," is of like quality with that of the three reapers. Do what we will, our imagination cannot transcend the stalwart strength of thews and sinews. We can clothe this strength with grace, gift it with ethereal charm, inspire it with ideal fancy, wrap it around in religious mystery. But the beautiful, strong body of the man remains the central fact for art. In like manner, the spirit of Christ revives in the poor, ugly drudge, "despised and rejected of men," like Paul " of presence weak, of speech contemptible," who devotes his substance and his time to support and, if possible, to save an erring brother.

This piercing through gauds and trimmings, this unmasking and unbaring of appearances, this recognition of divinity in all things, is the secret of the democratic spirit. It is not altogether different from what Jesus meant when he said : "Inasmuch as ye have done it to one of the least of these, ye do it unto me." Nor does the supreme doctrine of redemption through self-sacrifice and suffering lose in significance if we extend it from One, imagined a pitiful and condescending God, to all who for a worthy cause have endured humiliation, pain, an agonising death. Not to make Christ less, but to make him the chief of a multitude, the type and symbol of triumphant heroism, do we think of the thousands who have died on battle-fields, in torture-chambers, at the stake, from lingering misery, as expiators and redeemers, in whom the lamp of the divine spirit shines clearly for those who have the eyes to see.

This exposition of democracy shows that Whitman regarded it not merely as a political phenomenon, but far more as a form of religious enthusiasm. That being the case, his treatment of democracy includes far-reaching speculations on the literature and art required by the sovereign people, on the creation of national character, and on the proper place of what is called culture in a noble scheme of public education.

These problems have so vital an importance for England and Europe, as well as for America, that it will be well to discuss them fully, and to see what assistance toward their solution can be found in Whitman's writings.

There are two aspects under which the problem of democratic art must be regarded. In the first place, we have to ask what sort of art, including literature under this title, democracy requires. To this question Whitman, in his " Democratic Vistas," gives an answer : turbid in expression, far from lucid, but pregnant with sympathetic intelligence of the main issues. In the second place, we have to ask what elements are furnished to the artist by the people, which have not already been worked out in the classical and feudal forms and their derivatives. Whitman attempts to supply us with an answer to this second question also, not in his speculative essays, but in the mass of imaginative compositions which he designates by the name of poems or notes for poems. His report upon both topics may be postponed for the moment, while we revert to the revolution effected by the romantic movement of a hundred years ago. It behoves us to review the clearance of obsolete obstructions, and to survey the new ground gained, whereon our hopes are founded of a future reconstruction.

Delivered from scholastic traditions regarding style and the right subjects to be handled—delivered from pedantry and blind reactionary fervour—delivered from dependence upon aristocratic and ecclesiastical authority—sharing the emancipation of the intellect by modern science and the enfranchisement of the individual by new political conceptions—the poet or the artist is brought immediately face to face with the wonderful fresh world of men and things he has to interpret and to recreate. The whole of nature, seen for the first time with sane eyes, the whole of humanity, liberated for the first time from caste and class distinctions, invite his sympathy. Now dawns upon his mind the beauty, the divinity, which lies enfolded in the simplest folk, the commonest objects presented to his senses. He perceives the dignity of humble occupations, the grace inherent in each kind of labour well performed. He discovers that love is a deity in the cottage no less than in king's chambers; not with the supercilious condescension of Tasso's "Aminta" or Guarini's "Pastor Fido," but with a reverent recognition of the *præsens deus* in the heart of every man and woman. In order to make Florizel and Perdita charming, it is no longer necessary that they should be prince and princess in disguise; nor need the tale of "Daphnis and Chloe" now be written with that lame conclusion of lost children restored to wealthy high-born parents. Heroism steps forth from the tent of Achilles; chivalry descends from the arm-gaunt charger of the knight; loyalty is seen to be no mere devotion to a dynasty; passionate friendship quits the brotherhood of Pylades and the dear embraces of Peirithous. None of these high virtues belonging to heroic and chivalrous society are lost to us. On the contrary, we find them everywhere. They are brought within reach, instead of being relegated to some remote region in the past, or deemed the special property of privileged classes. The engine-driver steering his train at night over perilous viaducts, the lifeboat man, the member of a fire-brigade assailing houses toppling to their ruin among flames; these are found to be no less heroic than Theseus grappling the Minotaur in Cretan labyrinths. And so it is with the chivalrous respect for womanhood and weakness, with loyal self-dedication to a principle or cause, with comradeship uniting men in brotherhood, with passion fit for tragedy, with beauty shedding light from heaven on human habitations. They were thought to dwell far off in antique fable or dim mediæval legend. They appeared to our fancy clad in glittering armour, plumed and spurred, surrounded with the aureole of noble birth. We now behold them at our house-doors, in the streets and fields around us. Conversely, our eyes are no longer shut to the sordidness and baseness which royal palaces and princely hearts may harbour—to the meanness of the Court of the Valois, to the vulgarity of the Court of Charles II., to the vile tone of a Prince Regent, to the dishonour, dishonesty, and disloyalty toward women which have always, more or less, prevailed in so-called good society.

This extended recognition of the noble and the lovely qualities in human life, the qualities upon which pure poetry and art must seize, is due partially to what we call democracy. But it implies something more than that word is commonly supposed to denote—a new and more deeply religious way of looking at mankind, a gradual triumph after so many centuries of the spirit which is Christ's, an enlarged faculty for piercing below externals and appearances to the truth and essence of things. God, the divine, is recognised as immanent in nature, and in the soul and body of humanity; not external to these things, not conceived of as creative from outside, or as incarnated in any single personage, but as all-pervasive, all-constitutive, everywhere, and inspiring all. That is the democratic philosophy; and science has contributed in no small measure to produce it.

Meanwhile, we need not preach the abandonment of high time-honoured themes. Why should we seek to break the links which bind us to the best of that far past from which we came? Achilles has not ceased to be a fit subject for poem or statue, because we discern heroism in an engine-driver. Lovely knights and Flora Macdonald, Peirithous and Pylades, King Cophetua and Burd Helen, abide with all the lustre of their strength and grace and charm. They have lost nothing because others have gained—because we now acknowledge that the chivalry, the loyalty, the comradeship, the love, the pathos, which made their stories admirable, are shared by living men and women, whose names have not been sounded through fame's silver trumpet.

I have hitherto touched but lightly upon the extension of the sphere of beauty which may be expected from democratic art. Through it we shall be led to discover the infinite varieties of lovely form which belong peculiarly to the people. Caste and high birth have no monopoly of physical comeliness. It may even be maintained that social conditions render it impossible for them to display more than a somewhat limited range of beauty. Goethe, I think, defined good society as that which furnished no material for poetry. We might apply this paradox to plastic art, and say that polished gentlemen and ladies do not furnish the best materials for sculpture and painting. How hardly shall they who wear evening clothes and ball-dresses enter into the kingdom of the grandest plastic art! The sculpture of Pheidias, the fresco of Buonarroti, demand suggestions from the body, indications of the nude. The sublimest attitudes of repose imply movements determined by specific energy. There is a characteristic beauty in each several kind of diurnal service, which waits to be elucidated. The superb poise of the mower, as he swings his scythe ; the muscles of the blacksmith, bent for an unerring stroke upon the anvil ; the bowed form of the reaper, with belt tightened round his loins ; the thresher's arm uplifted, while he swings the flail ; the elasticity of oarsmen rising from their strain against the wave ; the jockey's grip across his saddle ; the mountaineer's slow, swinging stride ; the girl at the spinning-wheel, or carrying the water-bucket on her head, or hanging linen on the line, or busied with her china-closet : in each and every motive of this kind—and the list might be indefinitely prolonged, for all trades and occupations have some distinguishing peculiarity—there appears a specific note of grace inalienable from the work performed The artists of previous ages did not wholly neglect this truth. Indeed, they were eager to avail themselves of picturesque suggestions on the lines here indicated. Yet they used these motives mainly as adjuncts to themes of more attractive import, and subordinated them to what was deemed some loftier subject. Consequently, these aspects of life did not receive the attention they deserve; and the stores of beauty inherent in human industries have been only partially developed. It is the business of democratic art to unfold them fully. The time has come when the noble and beautiful qualities of the people demand a prominent place among worthy artistic motives.

An arduous task lies before poetry and the arts, if they are to bring themselves into proper relation with the people; not, as is vulgarly supposed, because the people will debase their standard, but because it will be hard for them to express the real dignity, and to satisfy the keen perceptions and the pure taste of the people.

There is a danger lest the solution of this problem should suffer from being approached too consciously. What we want is simplicity, emotional directness, open-mindedness, intelligent sympathy, keen and yet reverent curiosity, the scientific combined with the religious attitude toward fact. It will not do to be doctrinaire or didactic. Patronage and condescension are the worst of evils here. The spirit of Count Tolstoi, if that could descend in some new Pentecost, would prepare the world for democratic art.

Above all things, the middle-class conception of life must be transcended. Decency, comfort, sobriety, maintenance of appearances, gradual progression up a social ladder which is scaled by tenths of inches, the chapel or the church, the gig or the barouche, the growing balance at one's bankers, the addition of esquire to our name or of a red rosette to our button-hole, the firm resolve to keep well abreast with next-door neighbours, if not ahead of them, in business and respectability—all these things, which characterise the middle-class man wherever he appears, are good in their way. It were well that the people should incorporate these virtues. But there are corresponding defects in the *bourgeoisie* which have to be steadily rejected—an unwillingness to fraternise, an incapacity for comradeship, a habit of looking down on so-called inferiors, a contempt for hand-labour, a confusion of morality with prejudice and formula, a tendency to stifle religion in the gas of dogmas and dissenting shibboleths, an obstinate insensibility to ideas. Snobbery and Pharisaism, in one form or another, taint the middle-class to its core. Self-righteousness and personal egotism and ostrich-fear corrode it. We need to deliver our souls from these besetting sins, and to rise above them into more ethereal atmosphere. The man of letters, the artist, who would fain prove himself adequate to democracy in its noblest sense, must emerge from earthy vapours of complacent self and artificial circumstance and decaying feudalism. It is his privilege to be free, and to represent freedom. It is his function to find a voice or mode of utterance, an ideal of form, which shall be on a par with nature delivered from unscientific canons of interpretation, and with mankind delivered from obsolescent class-distinctions.

The most perplexing branch of the inquiry has to be affronted, when we ask the question: What kind of literature and art is demanded by democracy? How is art to prove its power by satisfying the needs and moral aspirations of the people who are sovereign in a democratic age?

The conditions under which art exists at the present time render a satisfactory answer to this question well-nigh impossible. In the past epochs, Greek, Mediæval, Italian, Elizabethan, Louis XIV., Persian, Japanese, the arts had a certain unconscious and spontaneous *rapport* with the nations which begat them, and with the central life-force of those nations at the moment of their flourishing. Whether that central energy was aristocratic, as in Hellas; or monarchic, as in France; or religious, as in mediæval Europe; or intellectual, as in Renaissance Italy; or national, as in Elizabethan England; or widely diffused like a fine gust of popular intelligence, as in Japan; signified comparatively little. Art expressed what the people had of noblest and sincerest, and was appreciated by the people. No abrupt division separated the nation from the poets who gave a voice to the nation. The case is altered now. On the one hand we have huge uncultivated populations, trained to mechanical industries and money-making, aggregated in unwieldy cities or distributed over vast tracts of imperfectly subdued territory, composed of heterogeneous racial elements, the *colluvies omnium gentium*, reduced by commerce and science and politics to a complex of shrewdly-acting, keenly-trafficking, dumbly-thinking personalities, bound together by superficial education in the commonest rudiments of knowledge, without strong national notes of difference, and without any specific bias toward a particular form of self-expression. On the other hand we have cosmopolitan men of letters, poets, painters, sculptors, architects, living for the most part upon the traditions of the past, working these up into new shapes of beauty with power and subtlety, but taking no direct hold on the masses, of whom they are contentedly ignorant, manifesting in no region of the world a marked national type of utterance, embodying no religion in their work, destined apparently to bequeath to the future an image of the nineteenth century in its confused Titanic energy, diffused culture, and mental chaos.

Is Democratic Art possible in these circumstances? Can we hope that the men who write poems, paint pictures, carve statues, shall enter once again into vital *rapport* with the people who compose the nations—the people who are now so far more puissant and important than they ever were before in the world's history? Is there to be any place for art in the real life of the future? Or are we about to realise the dream of Dupont in De Musset's satirical dialogue?

> Sur deux rayons de fer un chemin magnifique
> De Paris à Péking ceindra ma république.
> Là, cent peuples divers, confondant leur jargon,
> Feront une Babel d'un colossal wagon.
> Là, de sa roue en feu le coche humanitaire
> Usera jusqu'aux os les muscles de la terre.
> Du haut de ce vaisseau les hommes stupéfaits
> Ne verront qu'une mer de choux et de navets.
> Le monde sera propre et net comme une écuelle;
> L'humanitairerie en fera sa gamelle,
> Et le globe rasé, sans barbe ni cheveux,
> Comme un grand potiron roulera dans les cieux.

In a word, do the people, in this democratic age, possess qualities which are capable of evoking a great art from the sympathy of men of genius? Or is art destined to subside lower and lower into a kind of Byzantine decrepitude, as the toy of a so-called cultivated minority?

It is questionable whether Whitman will help us to see light in these perplexities. Yet he has a burning belief in democracy; and, what is more, he is one of the very few great writers of our epoch who was born among the people, who lived with the people, who understood and loved them thoroughly, and who dedicated his health and energies to their service in a time of overwhelming national anxiety.

Whitman was firmly persuaded that the real greatness of a nation or an epoch has never been, and can never be, tested by material prosperity. The wealth and strength, the mechanical industries, the expansive vigour, the superabundant population, of a State, constitute its body only. These will impose upon the world, control the present, and be a fact to reckon with for many generations. Yet these must eventually pass away, and sink into oblivion, unless the race attains to consciousness and noble spiritual life. Literature and art compose the soul which informs that colossal body with vitality, and which will continue to exist after the material forces of the race have crumbled into nothingness. Hellas lives ideally in Homer, Pheidias, Æschylus; Israel, in the Prophets and the Psalms; the Middle Ages, in Dante; Feudalism, in Shakespeare. But where is Phœnicia, where is Carthage? Nothing survives to symbolise their greatness, because they lacked ideas and ideal utterance.

In America, Whitman finds the material conditions of a puissant nation; but he does not find the spirit of a nation. The body is there, growing larger and grander every day, for ever acquiring fresh equipments and more powerful appliances. Meanwhile the soul, the ideality of art and literature, commensurate with this gigantic frame, is wanting.

Viewed, to-day, from a point of view sufficiently overarching, the problem of humanity all over the civilised world is social and religious, and is to be finally met and treated by literature. *The priest departs, the divine literatus comes.** Never was anything more wanted than, to-day, and here in The States, the poet of the modern is wanted, or the great literatus of the modern.†

* These and all other italics are mine; intended to direct attention to the main points as I conceive them, in my quotations from Whitman.
† This and the following extracts are taken from "Democratic Vistas."

What is our religion? he asks. "A lot of churches, sects, &c., the most dismal phantasms I know, usurp the name of religion."

What is our national prosperity? "The magician's serpent in the fable ate up all the other serpents: and money-making is our magician's serpent, remaining to-day sole master of the field."

What does our huge material expansion amount to? "It is as if we were somehow being endowed with a vast and more and more thoroughly appointed body, and then left with little or no soul."

What are our cities? "A sort of dry and flat Sahara appears—these cities crowded with petty grotesques, malformations, phantoms, playing meaningless antics."

What is our boasted culture? "Do you term that perpetual, pistareen, paste-pot work American art, American drama, taste, verse?" Instead of poets corresponding to the pitch and vigour of the race, he sees "a parcel of dandies and ennuyees, dapper little gentlemen from abroad, who flood us with their thin sentiment of parlours, parasols, piano-songs, tinkling rhymes, the five-hundredth importation, or whimpering and crying about something, chasing one aborted conceit after another, and for ever occupied in dyspeptic amours with dyspeptic women."*

After this fashion, with superfluous reiteration, and considerable asperity, Whitman pours forth his deep-felt conviction of America's spiritual inadequacy.

But what does he demand in lieu of those "most dismal phantasms, which usurp the name of religion"; in lieu of "the magician's serpent, money-making"; in lieu of the "Sahara of frivolous and petty cities"; in lieu of "paste-pot work," and "dapper little gentlemen," and "tinkling rhymes," and "dyspeptic amours"? Democracy in the cradle, in its stronghold, as it seems, is infected with these congenital diseases. Let us attempt to analyse what he proposes, and how he thinks the vital forces of the future are to be developed.

Whitman maintains that the cardinal elements

* "Dyspeptic amours with dyspeptic women," is a fine motto for the American Society novel. So is another of Whitman's phrases: "The sly settee and the adulterous, unwholesome couple," for the modern French novel.

of national greatness are robust character, independent personality, sincere religiousness. He contends that the democratic idea, properly grasped, and systematically applied to conduct, will suffice to reconstitute society upon a sound basis, and to supply the modern nations with the ideality they lack.

Of all this, and these lamentable conditions, to breathe into them the breath recuperative of sane and heroic life, I say a new founded literature, not merely to copy and reflect existing surfaces, or pander to what is called taste—not only to amuse, pass away time, celebrate the beautiful, the refined, the past, or exhibit technical, rhythmic, or grammatical dexterity—but a *literature underlying life, religious, consistent with science, handling the elements and forces with competent power, teaching and training men*—and, as perhaps the most precious of its results, achieving the redemption of woman out of those incredible holds and webs of silliness, millinery, and every kind of dyspeptic depletion—and thus insuring to The States a strong and sweet female race, a race of perfect mothers—is what is needed.

In culture, as it at present exists, the forces are alien and antagonistic to democracy. Therefore Whitman attacks it vigorously in a long polemical argument:

Dominion strong is the body's; dominion stronger is the

mind's. What has filled, and fills to-day our intellect, our fancy, furnishing the standards therein, is yet foreign. The great poems—Shakespeare included—are poisonous to the idea of the pride and dignity of the common people, the life-blood of Democracy. The models of our literature, as we get it from other lands, ultramarine, have had their birth in courts, and basked and grown in castle sunshine; all smells of princes' favours. Of workers of a certain sort, we have, indeed, plenty, contributing after their kind; many elegant, many learned, all complacent. But, touched by the national test, or tried by the standards of Democratic personality, they wither to ashes. I say I have not seen a single writer, artist, lecturer, or what not, that has confronted the voiceless, but ever erect and active, pervading, underlying will and typic aspiration of the land, in a spirit kindred to itself.

Culture is good enough in its way; but it is not what forms a manly personality, a sound and simple faith. "As now taught, accepted, and carried out, *are not the processes of culture rapidly creating a class of supercilious infidels, who believe in nothing?* Shall a man lose himself in countless masses of adjustments, and be so so shaped with reference to this, that, and the other, that the simply good and healthy, and brave parts of him are reduced and chipped away, like the bordering of box in a garden? You can cultivate corn and roses, and orchards; but who shall cultivate the primeval forests, the mountain peaks, the ocean, and the tumbling gorgeousness of the clouds? Lastly, is the readily given reply that culture only seeks to help, systematise, and put in attitude the elements of fertility and power, a conclusive reply?" The only culture useful to democracy is bound to aim less at polish and refinement of taste than at the bracing of character. "It must have for its spinal meaning *the formation of typical personality of character, eligible to the uses of the high average of men*— and not restricted by conditions ineligible to the masses. The best culture will always be that of the manly and courageous instincts, and loving perceptions, and of self-respect."

Since you cannot cultivate the primeval forests, and so forth, you must study and assimilate them. Since the people do not need to be refined in taste, but to be braced in character, you must penetrate their character and reproduce it in ideal conceptions. The right formative influences for modern literature and art have therefore to be sought in the people themselves; in the principles of independence and equality, of freedom, brotherhood, and comradeship, which are inherent in democracy, and by right of which democracy enfolds a religious ideal comparable to the spiritual liberty of the Gospel.

Did you, too, O friend, suppose Democracy was only for elections, for politics, or for a party name ? I say Democracy is only of use there that it may pass on and come to its flower and fruits in manners, in the highest forms of interaction between men, and their beliefs—in Religion, Literature, colleges and schools—Democracy in all public and private life, and in the Army and Navy. I have intimated that, as a paramount scheme, it has yet few or no full realisers and believers. I do not see, either, that it owes any serious thanks to noted propagandists or champions, or has been essentially helped, though often harmed, by them. . . . . It is not yet, there or anywhere, the fully received, the fervid, the absolute faith. I submit, therefore, that the fruition of Democracy on aught like a grand scale, resides altogether in the future.

Meanwhile, for those who believe that national greatness can only be tested by the spirit which a people manifests, it remains to fix attention firmly on the permanent and indestructible significance of arts and letters :

The literature, songs, æsthetics, &c., of a country *are of importance principally because they furnish the materials and suggestions of personality for the women and men of that country,* and enforce them in a thousand effective ways.

But what has culture, as yet, done to strengthen the personality of the millions of America?

When I mix with these interminable swarms of alert turbulent, good-natured, independent citizens, mechanics, clerks, young persons—at the idea of this mass of men, so fresh and free, so loving and so proud, a singular awe falls upon me. I feel, with dejection and amazement, that among our geniuses and talented writers or speakers, few or none have yet really spoken to this people, or created a single image-making work that could be called for them—or absorbed the central spirit and the idiosyncrasies which are theirs, and which, thus, in highest ranges, so far remain entirely uncelebrated, unexpressed.

Yet I have dreamed, merged in that hidden-tangled problem of our fate, whose long unravelling stretches mysteriously through time—dreamed out, portrayed, hinted already—a little or a larger band—a band of brave and true, unprecedented yet—armed and equipped at every point—the members separated, it may be, by different dates and states, or south or north, or east, or west—Pacific or Atlantic—a year, a century here, and other centuries there—but always one compact in soul, conscience-conserving, God-inculcating, inspired achievers, not only in Literature, the greatest art, but achievers in all art—a new, undying order, dynasty, from age to age transmitted—a band, a class, at least as fit to cope with current years, our dangers, needs, as those who, for their times, so well, in armour or in cowl, upheld and made illustrious, the feudal, priestly world. To offset chivalry, indeed, those vanquished countless knights, and the old altars, abbeys, all their priests, ages and strings of ages, a knightlier and more sacred cause to-day demands, and shall supply, in a New

World, to larger, grander work, more than the counterpart and tally of them.

So far I have followed Whitman in his polemic against the culture of his country and this century. Many of his prophetic utterances will appear inapplicable to Europe. Yet democracy, whether we like it or not, has to be faced and accepted in the Old as well as the New World. Here, therefore, as across the Atlantic, democracy is bound to produce an ideal of its own, or to "prove the most tremendous failure of time." Here, as there, "long enough have the people been listening to poems in which common humanity, deferential, bends low, humiliated, acknowledging superiors." And yet, here, as there, the people have arrived at empire. It is no longer possible to apostrophise them in the words of Campanella's famous sonnet:

> The people is a beast of muddy brain
> > That knows not its own strength, and therefore stands
> > Loaded with wood and stone; the powerless hands
> > Of a mere child guide it with bit and rein;
>
> One kick would be enough to break the chain;
> > But the beast fears, and what the child demands
> > It does; nor its own terror understands,
> > Confused and stupefied by bugbears vain.

Most wonderful! with its own hand it ties
    And gags itself—gives itself death and war
    For pence doled out by kings from its own store.
Its own are all things between earth and heaven ;
    But this it knows not ; and if one arise
    To tell this truth, it kills him unforgiven.

In Europe, again, as in America, the founts of earlier inspiration are failing. Classical antiquity and romance cannot supply perennial nutriment for modern art. The literary revolution which marked the advent of the romantic and the scientific genius, dethroned those elder deities and threw the sanctuary of the spirit open. Science, the sister of democracy, brings man face to face with nature, and with God in nature. A more ethereal spirituality than has yet been dreamed of begins to penetrate our conceptions of the universe, of law, of duty, of human rights and destinies. Art and literature, if they are to hold their own, must adapt themselves to these altered conditions. They must have a faith—not in their own excellence as art, and in their several styles and rhythms—but in their mission and their power to present the puissance of the age, its religion and its character, with the same force as the Greek sculptors presented paganism and the Italian painters presented mediæval catholicity. If they cannot ascend to this endeavour they are lost.

"Literature, strictly considered," says Whitman, "has never recognised the People, and, whatever may be said, does not to-day. . . . . I know nothing more rare, even in this country, than a fit scientific estimate and reverent appreciation of the People—*of their measureless wealth of latent power and capacity, their vast artistic contrasts of lights and shades*, with, in America, their entire reliability in emergencies, and a certain breadth of historic grandeur, of peace or war, far surpassing all the vaunted samples of book-heroes, or any *haut-ton* coteries, in all the records of the world."

This assertion he proceeds to support by reference to the great American War. "Probably no future age can know, but I well know, how the gist of this fiercest and most resolute of the world's warlike contentions resided exclusively in the unnamed, unknown rank and file; and how the brunt of its labour of death was, to all essential purposes, Volunteered." "Grand common stock! to me the accomplished and convincing growth, prophetic of the future; proof undeniable to sharpest sense *of perfect beauty, tenderness, and pluck*, that never feudal lord, nor Greek, nor Roman breed yet rivalled."

We now understand what Whitman means by "the divine average"; why he exclaims: "Ever the most precious in the common. Ever the fresh breeze of field, or hill, or lake is more than any palpitation of fans, though of ivory, and redolent with perfume; and the air is more than the costliest perfumes."

Finally, something must be said about Whitman's attitude towards the past. His polemic against contemporary culture, his firm insistence upon the fact that "the mind, which alone builds the permanent edifice, haughtily builds *for itself*," and that consequently a great nation like America, a new principle like Democracy, is bound to find its own ideal expression or " to prove the most tremendous failure of time"—all this may blind us to his reverence for the arts and literatures of races and of ages which have passed away. How easy it would be to assume a contempt for history in Whitman is clear enough to students of his writings. From the pages which he dedicates to the use and value of bygone literatures it will be sufficient to extract the following paragraph:

> Gathered by geniuses of city, race, or age, and put by them in the highest of art's forms, namely, the literary form, the peculiar combinations, and the outshows of that city, race, and age, its particular modes of the universal attributes and passions, its faiths, heroes, lovers and gods, wars, traditions, struggles, crimes, emotions, joys (or the subtle spirit of these), having been passed on to us to illumine our own selfhood and its experiences—what they supply, indispensable and highest, if taken away, *nothing else in all the world's boundless storehouses could make up to us or ever return again.*

This is an emphatic re-assertion of the principle that "dominion strong is the body's; dominion stronger is the mind's." Not for an age or nation, but for all humanity and all time, abides the truth that material strength and greatness are but bone, and thew, and sinew; literature and art constitute the soul. Therefore the prophets, poets, thinkers, builders, sculptors, painters, musicians of past ages and of foreign lands, abide imperishable, shining like suns and stars fixed in the firmament of man's immortal mind. Stupendous are they, indeed, but distant, unfamiliar; appealing indirectly to modern hearts and brains. Our admiration for them, the use we make of them, the lessons we learn from them, must not degrade us into the frivolity of imitative culture. We have to bear steadfastly in mind that it is our duty to emulate them by creating corresponding monuments of our own spirit, suns and stars which shall shine with them " in the spaces of that other heaven, the kosmic intellect, the soul."

Ye powerful and resplendent ones! ye were, in your atmospheres, grown not for America, but rather for her foes, the feudal and the old—while our genius is Democratic and modern. Yet could ye, indeed, but breathe your breath of life into our New World's nostrils—not to enslave us, as now, but, for our needs, to breed a spirit like your own—perhaps (dare we say it?) to dominate, even destroy, what yourselves have left! On your plane, and no less, but even higher and wider, will I meet and measure for our wants to-day and here. I demand races of orbic bards, with unconditional, uncompromising sway. Come forth, sweet democratic despots of the west!

Thus, the upshot of Walt Whitman's message is that the people, substantial as they are, and full of all the qualities which might inspire a world-literature, have up to the present time found no representative in poetry and art. The *sacer vates* of democracy has not appeared. "The fruition of Democracy, on aught like a grand scale, resides altogether in the future."

This is not the place to inquire how far Whitman has himself fulfilled the conditions of writing for the people. Judged by his acceptance in America, he can hardly be said to have succeeded in his own lifetime. The many-headed beast there, if it has not literally "trampled him in gore," turns a deaf ear to his voice, and treats him with comparative indifference. Hitherto he has won more respect from persons of culture in Great Britain than from the divine average of The States.

VII

WHEN, at the age of thirty-five, Whitman resolved "to strike up the songs of the New World," he had formed the opinion that America—and America, as we have seen, with him is equivalent to Democracy—demanded a wholly new type of poetry. It would not do for the poet to go on using the rhymes and metres and stanzas which had become stale in the Old World, and were being imitated by feeble folk of culture on the other side of the Atlantic. Themes so vast, a people so gigantic, a future so illimitable, called for corresponding forms of artistic expression. But, what was most important, the would-be poet had to assume a new attitude towards literature, and to regard his duties with a different kind of seriousness.

The first edition of "Leaves of Grass" appeared in 1855, after two years of anxious preparation. It is a thin quarto volume, containing a few of

Whitman's most important poems, and a long prose preface. In the preface, which is remarkable for fervid eloquence and cultivated thought, he expressed his theory of the poetry adapted to Democracy and America. The germ of all his subsequent work, with the exception of "Calamus," may be found in this pregnant essay, and not a few of his later poems are simple expansions of its themes. Here, then, we have in a condensed form what may be called his "poetics." At the same time, those first essays in poetical literature which followed—especially the long piece afterwards entitled "Walt Whitman"—gave a sample of the manner in which he intended to carry his doctrines into practice. That he was seriously attempting to create a new style for America, and to suggest, at any rate, what might be left for other bards to perfect, appears from the preface to the edition of 1872. Here he says: "The impetus and ideas urging me, for some years past, to an utterance, or attempt at utterance, of New World songs, and an epic of Democracy, having already had their published expression, as well as I can expect to give it, in 'Leaves of Grass,' the present and future pieces from me are really but the surplusage forming after that volume, or the wave eddying behind it." His main object had, in fact, been attained when the edition of 1867, including "Drum Taps," appeared.

Later on, in the preface of 1872, he adds: "I have been more anxious, anyhow, to suggest the songs of vital endeavour and manly evolution, and furnish something for races of outdoor athletes, than to make perfect rhymes, or reign in the parlours. I ventured from the beginning in my own way, taking chances, and would keep on venturing."

Following the prose manifesto of 1855, and taking it paragraph by paragraph, we may now discuss Whitman's conception of the ideal Democratic bard, and pause from time to time to consider how closely he approached his own standard. He begins with a panegyric of America, which is certainly justified by the largeness of that continent, the variety of climates it includes, and the teeming populations who inhabit it. Still, methinks, the eagle screams too loudly, the "barbaric yawp" is too apparent in this opening strain of jubilation. The Americans may, indeed, be destined to be "the race of races"; but hitherto they have done mighty little for the furtherance of spirituality, being principally occupied with commercial speculation, wire-pulling at elections, and doubtful doings in Wall Street. For aught they have as yet achieved, it is possible that they will never get further than Carthage of old did. When we reflect what " the small theatre of the antique, and the aimless sleep-walking of the Middle Ages," to use Whitman's words, bequeathed to us of spiritual revelations, and compare these with the null or zero of American productivity, we could have preferred a more becoming modesty, or a salutary depression, at the outset. But that is not Whitman's opinion. He has a firm faith in national personality, and is not daunted by the poverty of national attainment.* And, as we have already seen, he elsewhere confesses that the democratic bard has not appeared.

---

* It is right to add that at the close of his life, in conversation with J. W. Wallace, he observed : " There is nowhere in the world the demonism, the foulness, the corruption we have here in America. I know that the average bulk *en masse* is sound. But this is the danger."

The first great quality of the bard is faith. " The times straying toward infidelity and confections and persiflage he withholds by steady faith." He will find a responsive virtue in the proletariate. " Faith is the antiseptic of the soul—it pervades the common people and preserves them, they never give up believing, and expecting, and trusting. There is that indescribable freshness and unconsciousness about an illiterate person that mocks the power of the noblest expressive genius."

The second great quality of the bard is simplicity and candour. He must recognise the fact that others can perceive beauty as well as he does, but that it is his duty to seize upon the facts of the universe and to reveal their inner life, the abiding relations they contain. It is not merely his duty to see, and to invest what he has seen with rhymes and rhetorical ornaments, but to realise, and to present what he has realised, with flawless accuracy. " Without effort, and without exposing in the least how it is done, the greatest poet brings the spirit of any, or all, events, and passions, and scenes, and persons, some more and some less, to bear on your individual character as you hear or read. To do this well is to compete with the laws that pursue and follow time." Therefore the poet of Democracy will not stop at description or the epic. His expression is to be "transcendent and new, indirect and not direct." What that means, Whitman has more fully set forth in the poem called "Introductions," where he contrasts the mere singer with the real poet.

> The words of the singers are the hours or minutes of the light or dark—but the words of the maker of poems are the general light and dark;
>
> The maker of poems settles justice, reality, immortality,
> His insight and power encircle things and the human race,
> He is the glory and extract, thus far, of things, and of the human race.
>
> The singers do not beget—only the Poet begets.

Thus it appears that the distinctive faculty of the bard is intuition into the essential realities, penetrative imagination, combined with the power of communicating what he has discovered of vital truth through words. His relation toward the mere singer is that of the Imagination to the Fancy.

The advice given by Whitman to one who

would place himself in the proper attitude for making poems, and presumably also for comprehending them when made, is contained in the following characteristic paragraph.

This is what you shall do: Love the earth and sun and the animals, despise riches, give alms to every one that asks, stand up for the stupid and crazy, devote your income and labour to others, hate tyrants, argue not concerning God, have patience and indulgence toward the people, take off your hat to nothing known or unknown, or to any man or number of men—go freely with powerful uneducated persons and with the young, and with the mothers of families—re-examine all you have been told in school or church or in any book, and dismiss whatever insults your own soul; and your very flesh shall be a great poem, and have the richest fluency, not only in its words, but in the silent lines of its lips and face, and between the lashes of your eyes, and in every motion and joint of your body. The poet shall not spend his time in unneeded work. He shall know that the ground is already plough'd and manured; others may not know it, but he shall. He shall go directly to the creation. His trust shall master the trust of everything he touches—and shall master all attachment.

The next great quality of the bard is a recognition of equality. "The messages of great poems to each man and woman are, come to us on equal terms, only then can you understand us. We are no better than you, what we enclose you enclose, what we enjoy, you may enjoy." He will be "marked for generosity and affection, and for encouraging competitors." Liberal and open to all influences, according preference to no one class, no special subject, no single element of the State.

The bard will not be intimidated by exact science, but will find in it "always his encouragement and support." Before his enlightened eyes the supernatural "departs as a dream." It is only nature, life, the body, the soul, that exhibit miracles; and these miracles are ever-recurrent, innumerable. Humanity must be studied and represented as it is, not as it ought to be according to some preconceived canon of perfection. It must be recognised that God is ultimately responsible for everything we discover in the universe. "Whatever would put God in a poem or system of philosophy as contending against some being or influence, is of no account."

Furthermore, following the same line of thought, fiction and romance disappear before "genuineness." "As soon as histories are properly told, no more need of romances." The actual beauty of the human form is superior to wayward creations of the plastic fancy. There is no pleasure, no joy, beyond that which a healthy soul in a healthy body may daily make its own. The poet will show that riches do not place their possessor at an advantage with regard to real pleasure, real joy; that the ownership of an extensive library does not enable a man to acquire intellectual stores of happiness beyond the scope of any one who can open and read the books; that to be the master of a park, a forest, a picture-gallery, will not help an insensible person to relish natural or æsthetic beauty. Any one who passes through the park, the gallery, the forest, with eyes to see and senses to perceive, is more the owner of them than their purchaser, if peradventure he be a dullard.

Another main requisite of the bard is "the idea of political liberty." Poets "are the voice and exhibition of liberty." Since the bard in question is the Bard of Democracy, this amounts to an identical proposition, and requires no comment. In this connection, however, I may note that the poet has to make himself familiar with the whole of America—its lands, rivers, lakes, fauna, flora, men and women, trades, arts, occupations, &c.— and also to "flood himself with the immediate age as with vast oceanic tides. If he be not himself the age transfigured, and if to him is not opened the eternity which gives similitude to all periods, and locations, and processes, and animate and inanimate forms, and which is the bond of time, and rises up from its inconceivable vagueness and infiniteness in the swimming shapes of to-day, and is held by the ductile anchors of life, and makes the present spot the passage from what was to what shall be, and commits itself to the representation of this wave of an hour, and this one of the sixty beautiful children of the wave, let him merge in the general run, and wait his development."

Then follows a very curious passage regarding the fundamental constituents of the true bard, which must be transcribed in the author's words:

Extreme caution or prudence, the soundest organic health, large hope and comparison and fondness for women and children, large alimentiveness and destructiveness and causality, with a perfect sense of the oneness of nature, and the propriety of the same spirit applied to human affairs, are called up of the float of the brain of the world to be parts of the greatest poet from his birth out of his mother's womb, and from her birth out of her mother's.

There are so many different things, and apparently

so disparate, jumbled together in this sentence that it offers hopeless difficulties to the commentator. We understand indeed what Whitman means by health, alimentiveness, even destructiveness. But how are these qualities combined with causality ? Then, again, hope and a fondness for women and children are intelligible. But why are they coupled with comparison ? [It looks almost as though causality and comparison were borrowed from the jargon of phrenology.] What is meant by a sense of the oneness of nature, and the application of nature's lessons to human affairs, has already been explained above. For the rest, as regards caution or prudence, Whitman in what follows offers a noble interpretation. " Caution seldom goes far enough. It has been thought that the prudent citizen was the citizen who applied himself to solid gains, and did well for himself and his family, and completed a lawful life without debt or crime." Whitman, like Christ in the Gospels, points out that this man is in reality very imprudent.

Beyond the independence of a little sum laid aside for burial-money, and of a few clap-boards around and shingles overhead on a lot of American soil own'd, and the easy dollars that supply the year's plain clothing and meals, the melancholy prudence of the abandonment of such a great being as a man is, to the toss and pallor of years of money-making, with all their scorching days and icy nights, and all their stifling deceits and underhand dodgings, or infinitesimals of parlours, or shameless stuffing while others starve, and all the loss of the bloom and odour of the earth, and of the flowers and atmosphere, and of the sea, and of the true taste of the women and men you pass or have to do with in youth or middle age, and the issuing sickness and desperate revolt at the close of a life without elevation or *naïveté* (even if you have achiev'd a secure 10,000 a year, or election to Congress or the Governorship), and the ghastly clatter of a death without serenity or majesty, is the great fraud upon modern civilisation and forethought, blotching the surface and system which civilisation undeniably drafts, and moistening with tears the immense features it spreads and spreads with such velocity before the reach'd kisses of the soul.

Thus extreme caution or prudence consists in living for the soul, immortality, the life beyond the grave, the constitution of a permanent and noble spiritual self, the eternal things and abiding relations of the universe. It is, in fact, what Whitman means by religion; and since we have returned to this which was the starting-point of our inquiry, I cannot refrain from inserting here a long paragraph (from the Preface, 1872), in which he expounds at length his views regarding the religion of the future:

When I commenced, years ago, elaborating the plan of my poems, and continued turning over that plan, and shifting it in my mind through many years (from the age of twenty-eight to thirty-five), experimenting much, and writing and abandoning much, one deep purpose underlay the others, and has underlain it and its execution ever since—and that has been the religious purpose. Amid many changes, and a formulation taking far different shape from what I at first supposed, this basic purpose has never been departed from in the composition of my verses. Not of course to exhibit itself in the old ways, as in writing hymns or psalms with an eye to the church-pew or to express conventional pietism, or the sickly yearnings of devotees, but in new ways, and aiming at the widest sub-bases and inclusions of humanity, and tallying the fresh air of sea and land. I will see (said I to myself) whether there is not, for my purposes as poet, a religion, and a sound religious germenancy in the average human race, at least in their modern development in the United States, and in the hardy common fibre and native yearnings and elements, deeper and larger, and affording more profitable returns than all mere sects or churches—as boundless, joyous, and vital as Nature itself—a germenancy that has too long been unencouraged, unsung, almost unknown. With science, the old theology of the East, long in its *dotage*, begins evidently to die and disappear. But (to my mind) science—and maybe such will prove its principal service—as evidently prepares the way for One indescribably grander—Time's young but perfect offspring—the new theology—heir of the West—lusty and loving, and wondrous beautiful. For America, and for to-day, just the same as any day, the supreme and final science is the science of God —what we call science being only its minister—as Democracy is, or shall be also. And a poet of America (I said) must fill himself with such thoughts, and chant his best out of them. And as those were the convictions and aims, for good or bad, of "Leaves of Grass," they are no less the intention of this volume. As there can be, in my opinion, no sane and complete personality, nor any grand and electric nationality, without the stock element of religion imbuing all the other elements (like heat in chemistry, invisible itself, but the life of all visible life), so there can be no poetry worthy the name without that element behind all. The time has certainly come to begin to discharge the idea of religion in the United States from mere ecclesiasticism, and from Sundays and churches and church-going, and assign it to that general position, chiefest and most indispensable, most exhilarating, to which the others are to be adjusted, inside of all human character and education and affairs. The people, especially the young men and women, of America, must begin to learn that religion (like poetry) is something far, far different from what they supposed. It is, indeed, too important to the power and perpetuity of the New World to be consign'd any longer to the churches, old or new, Catholic or Protestant —Saint this, or Saint that. It must be consign'd henceforth to Democracy *en masse*, and to literature. It must enter into the poems of the nation. It must make the nation.

VIII

SPEAKING broadly then, Whitman's conception of the ideal Bard of Democracy implies the following main qualities or properties. He must be possessed of perfect physical health, and the normal appetites and instincts. He must be in large and vital sympathy with his own nation and his own age. He must have illimitable faith and optimistic confidence. He must comprehend the heart of the people, recognise their nobility, base his trust in the future upon their sterling virtues and their spirituality. He must be a passionate lover of liberty, a believer in the equality of all men and women as regards their capacity for comprehending and enjoying what he comprehends and enjoys. He must derive his aliment and inspiration from science, nature, fact; aiming at truth and candour; preferring the genuine to the fictitious ; denying the supernatural, and finding the only divine known to us in things submitted to our percipient senses. The final result of this attitude will be to make him religious in a higher and intenser degree than any creed or dogma yet has made a man to be. As regards his special function in literature, he must be gifted with imagination penetrative to the soul and life of fundamental realities, and in his expression must be as simple, as suggestive, as inevitable, as a natural object. He will aim at creating a new and independent vehicle of language, suitable to the quality of his personal perception.

That Whitman described himself in this ideal picture of the bard—or rather, perhaps, that he strenuously attempted to live up to the conception he had formed, and to exemplify his teaching in his published works—will be apparent to all who have studied him with attention. With regard to physical health, Whitman, when he composed " Leaves of Grass," was almost repulsively and obtrusively healthy. After the experiences of the war, his health failed ; but though there entered a certain wistfulness and subdued tone into his poetry at this period, he never altered its form. " His self-assertion," as Mr. W. M. Rossetti observed, " is boundless ;

yet not always to be understood as strictly or merely personal to himself, but sometimes as vicarious, the poet speaking on behalf of all men, and every man and woman." That is well said. The "I" of Whitman is not merely his particular "Ego," but also the "personality" of that "Democratic Individual" he strove to create, and endowed with vocal organs. All the same, it must be admitted that the utterances of the ideal "self" would have been more solemn and more impressive, if Whitman had pitched them at a somewhat lower tone. He screams, brags, swears, blusters, asseverates, bullies, thumps the pulpit-cushion, stamps the platform. And all this "blatant ebullience," as it has been well described, indicates "a fault of debility, not an excess of strength." The worst thing, and the most obvious, which can be said against "Leaves of Grass" is that it is throughout impaired by forcible-feebleness. Partly due, no doubt, to the doctrinaire attitude assumed by the author as the would-be prophet of a new gospel and the founder of a new method. Partly due, also, to the arrogance of the athletic temperament. We cannot but regret that this accent of swagger had not been toned down, since it remains in permanent discord with the essential sublimity of Whitman's thought, the grandeur of his imagination, and the not unfrequent magnificence of his diction.

In all the other qualities of the democratic bard, Walt Whitman cannot be said to have fallen far short of his own ideal. For expressing America, the length, and breadth, and vastness of "These States," he was well equipped by the "Wander-jahren" of his earlier manhood. During those years of travel and of varied energy he practised many arts and crafts, and came into close relations with all kinds of men and women. If not in actual excesses, at any rate by sympathy and observation, he "sounded all experiences of life, with all their passions, pleasures, and abandonments." He felt the pulse of that enormous and promiscuous nationality. He fraternised with the people, not in his birth-place merely, nor in New England or New York, but in the South, the West, studying all types, selecting from each class of workers and of able craftsmen those characteristics which he afterwards fused into his "Democratic Individual." It was inevitable that he should leave certain salient qualities out of his account, and that the ideal portrait should be defective in some softening and spiritually elevating traits; for no man, sincerely studying nature and the world, can avoid the necessity under which he lies of importing his own predilections, proclivities, personal instincts into the amalgam of his art. For the completion of this task there never failed in Whitman large and liberal sympathies, the recognition of truth and goodness, wheresoever to be found, hearty love, affection of the purest, willingness to share on equal terms with all his fellows, to learn from the simplest, to discern divinity in the most abject, to place himself upon the level of "the average," and to ascend therefrom (as Antæus rose from contact with Mother Earth) inspired, invigorated, able to affront the stars and commune with the thought of death. Should a Hercules of culture, or of any superior creed, be sent to strangle Whitman, the demigod will have to lift him high in air above that vital contract with the ground-pan of humanity. His secret as a democratic bard lies in this living and unselfish love of man, body and soul, bred by a generous unenvious commerce with his kindred. The faith he preached as a saving and preservative virtue, and which he discovered, or seemed to discover, abroad among the people, abounded in his own breast. He was born with a robust confidence, and with imperturbable optimism. This believing and sanguine spirit survived, not only the experiences of his Wanderjahren, when he must have seen sad things enough to shake another's confidence, but also the dire events of the great war, the very saddest aspects of which he daily studied during his occupation as a hospital nurse. Inborn in the man, it was nourished and sustained by exact science—that is to say, by what he learned about the system of the universe, and by the interpretation he put upon that knowledge. Religion grew for him from roots which have proved poisonous to other souls. Herein, again, he showed his adequacy to his own conception of the poet. Faith and optimism prevailed against the manifold apparent inducements to despair of human nature, and to pronounce our world the worst possible product of some unconscious power for evil. The penetrative imagination he demanded from his poet enabled him to pierce the core of science, and to emerge from the contemplation of a homogeneous and everlastingly enduring universe into the conviction that no part of it can be destroyed or unaccounted for. That is no sentimental dream, no sybarite's self-indulgent escape from poignant realities of pain and misery into vague visions. It is the logical deduction from the facts of the world as science sets them forth, drawn by one who knows the world at least in one case to be good to live in, and who has thoroughly absorbed the meaning of its essential and coherent unity. As the test and pledge of Whitman's sincerity, the last period of his life—a life broken in the finest years of manhood by self-sacrifice for others during the Great War—remains for ever valuable. Instead of shrinking or quailing under the paralysis and poverty which afflicted him so long, his spirit rose and dilated. He never ceased to love and hope. The religion which he framed in ardent youth and arrogant adolescence, sustained him to the last. We have to be thankful that it was put to proof in this way, although we may have wished that one to whom the world owes so much had been spared suffering and privation. For no one now can say that Whitman's religion was the idle plaything of a lusty, omnivorously enjoying, morally careless, exceptionally fortunate child of nature. St. Paul spoke one of the deepest truths which have been ever uttered when he wrote : " And now abideth Faith, Hope, and Love, these three. But the greatest of these is Love." Whitman loved greatly, and sacrificed his life to the love he felt for suffering humanity. The orthodox Christian may go to Whitman in order to discover that the cardinal virtues can survive the decay of Christian dogma, and inspire one for whom the cosmic enthusiasm was the sole source of consolation.

IX

I WOULD fain close upon this note, for I have already declared what I feel to be incontestably great in Whitman. Yet it still remains to consider in what way he performed the bard's functions of initiating new forms in literature, and pioneering for an art commensurate with the magnificence of America.

Here it serves nothing to inquire whether he was justified in supposing that he had written poetry. It is clear that in a certain and technical sense he did not write poetry, because he did not use metre and rhyme. It is also clear that, except in his Prefaces, Democratic Vistas, Specimen Days, and so forth, he did not attempt to write prose. When he did write prose in "Leaves of Grass" and "Drum Taps," he did so involuntarily, and just as Dante in the "Paradiso," and Milton in the "Paradise Lost," and Lucretius in "De Rerum

Natura," unwillingly wrote prose at intervals. Therefore, it may be inferred—and one flings the suggestion with equanimity to cavillers— that what he did write in his masterpiece of literature was neither flesh nor fowl nor good red herring. It is not verse, it is not (except involuntarily) prose.

But is there no poetry outside the region of rhyme and verse? Was Sir Philip Sidney, the first accomplished critic in our language, so far wrong in his contention that "apparelled verse is but an ornament, and no cause to poetry; since there have been many most excellent poets that have never versified, and now swarm many versifiers who need never answer to the name of poets?" Are we all wrong in thinking that, when we read Job, the Psalms, the Prophets, the Song of Solomon, in our English version, we are reading the sublimest, the sweetest, the strongest, the most sensuous poetry that was ever written?

To my mind Whitman did indubitably produce poetry, and poetry of a very high order. According to the theory he had formed before he began to "strike up the songs of the New

World," he deliberately rejected rhyme, metre, the set stanza, all the " Ars Poetica" of his predecessors.* In art it is exceedingly difficult to break with tradition, to innovate with success. And doctrine, the obedience to a settled theory, is inimical to pure spontaneous singing. From the outset Whitman was hampered by his

* It must be remembered that Whitman protested against his works being judged from the point of view of "literature." He says moreover: " I have not only not bothered much about style, form, art, &c., but confess to more or less apathy (I believe I have sometimes caught myself in decided aversion) toward them throughout, asking nothing of them but negative advantages—that they should never impede me, and never under any circumstances, or for their own purposes only, assume any mastery over me." That is a sensible and intelligible account of his theory and practice. Yet he calls his collected works, "Complete Poems and Prose of Walt Whitman": he speaks of the former often as "Songs," "Chants," "Carols," and so forth. The critic is therefore compelled to treat them as products of art. But this is just what the disciples of Whitman do not like our doing. In a private letter to the aged master, his friend and biographer, Dr. Bucke, remarks concerning my "Essays Speculative and Suggestive" (in which there was an essay on Democratic Art, partly incorporated into this study) that "Symonds (like the rest) seems to be so mentally and unconsciously occupied with form that he is more or less blinded to substance." Mr. Robert Buchanan has told us that he was first attracted to Whitman because his work was not "mere literature," because he had broken with the tradition of artistic form. But, for all that, Whitman has form, a very peculiar and individual style, an art of expression which none of his followers—not even the genial Edward Carpenter, whose "Toward Democracy" is not only the best interpretation of Whitman's spirit, but also the best imitation of his manner—have been able to copy without enfeebling or parodying its characteristics.

system, and he was not quite strong enough to create by a single fiat the new perfect form he aimed at. He resolved to rely on rhythm, and on the coinage of phrases which should exactly suit the matter or the emotion to be expressed.

The countless clear and perfect [phrases he invented, to match most delicate and evanescent moods of sensibility, to picture exquisite and broad effects of natural beauty, to call up poignant or elusive feelings, attest to his artistic faculty of using language as a vehicle for thought. They are hung, like golden medals of consummate workmanship and incised form, in rich clusters over every poem he produced. And, what he aimed at above all, these phrases are redolent of the very spirit of the emotions they suggest, communicate the breadth and largeness of the natural things they indicate, embody the essence of realities in living words which palpitate and burn for ever.

I do not think it needful to quote examples. Those who demur and doubt may address themselves to an impartial study of his writings. It is enough for me, trained in Greek and Latin classics, in the literatures of Italy and France and Germany and England, who have spent my life in continuous addiction to literature, and who am the devotee of what is powerful and beautiful in style—it is enough for me to pledge my reputation as a critic upon what I have asserted.

I have already admitted that his self-assertion and tumidity are drawbacks to his art. Furthermore it must be confessed that the lists of things, of peoples, of places, he is wont to make, exhaust our powers of attention. We tire of uncouth paragraphs, each clause of which begins with "Oh," or "See," "I see," "I hear," "I swear," or "Shapes arise." We long for humour, which is almost totally absent in his work, to relieve its seriousness and self-complacency. We are jarred by his ungrammatical constructions and crude agglutinations of jaw-breaking substantives. His ill-assimilated French or Spanish phrases—imported in obedience to the system, because America includes so many nations— hurt our ear. We could gladly dispense with *etui, trottoir, habitans, eleve, allons, accouche, mon enfant,* and so forth, in compositions which after all are written in the English mother-tongue. Let us, however, be thankful that he did not think fit to borrow also from the German dictionary! Finally, we could desire more of dramatic power and a juster sense of composition in creating balanced wholes.

But when all this has been conceded, we return to the position, and declare it to be impregnable and unchallenged, that Whitman, working under the conditions of his chosen style, has produced long series of rhythmic utterances, strung together and governed by an inner law of melody, capable of transposition, augmentation, and diminution at the author's will, which have the magnetic charm of nature, the attraction of his own "fluid and attaching" personality.

In his happiest moments these periods are perfect poems, to alter which would be to ruin them. Not a word is then superfluous; not an epithet, but adds to the rhetorical effect; and when the climax is attained, our sense of music, and far more of vitalising imaginative potency, is fully satisfied.

Let those who doubt these words, or do not know Walt Whitman's writings, devote themselves to the careful study of " When Lilacs last in the Door-Yard Bloomed," " Vigil Strange I kept on the Field One Night," " The Singer in the Prison," " Sleep-Chasings," " A Leaf of Faces," " A Word Out of the Sea," and those passages from the poem called " Walt Whitman," which begin with the lines " I am he that walks with the tender and growing night," and " You sea ! I resign myself to you also."

X

I am aware how futile it is to attempt a full interpretation of Walt Whitman. There is something in him which eludes all efforts at description. No analytical process can be successfully, exhaustively applied to him. Nor is this the fault of his students and expositors. It springs from the quality of his work. As Colonel Ingersoll, his steadfast friend and eulogist, has said: "In everything a touch of chaos, lacking what is called form, as clouds lack form, but not lacking the splendour of sunrise or the glory of sunset." Then, too, there is a something in his poetry, the best of it, the spiritual essence, the ethereal, harmonising medium of its many incongruities, which evanesces in the crucible of criticism. It follows, therefore, that in writing of him every one has failed to introduce him adequately to the public. A blowing of the brazen trumpet, or a petty patronage, these are the two contradictory errors into which his well-wishers, even though they happen to be subtle writers, fail when they attempt to set forth what they feel about him.

I am not sure whether a loose, disjointed method, the mere jotting down of notes, would not be the best way of illustrating so intangible an author. And then I think of many metaphors to express a meaning irreducible to propositions.

He is Behemoth, wallowing in primeval jungles, bathing at fountain-heads of mighty rivers, crushing the bamboos and the crane-brakes under him, bellowing and exulting in the torrid air. He is a gigantic elk or buffalo, trampling the grasses of the wilderness, tracking his mate with irresistible energy. He is an immense tree, a kind of Ygdrasil, stretching its roots deep down into the bowels of the world, and unfolding its magic boughs through all the spaces of the heavens. His poems are even as the rings in a majestic oak or pine.* He is the circumambient air, in which float shadowy shapes, rise mirage-towers, and palm-groves ; we try to clasp their visionary

* Whitman said to J. W. Wallace : " I have felt to make my book a succession of growths, like the rings of trees."

forms; they vanish into ether. He is the globe itself; all seas, lands, forests, climates, storms, snows, sunshines, rains of universal earth. He is all nations, cities, languages, religions, arts, creeds, thoughts, emotions. He is the beginning and the grit of these things, not their endings, lees, and dregs. Then he comes to us as lover, consoler, physician, nurse; most tender, fatherly, sustaining those about to die, lifting the children, and stretching out his arms to the young men. What the world has he absorbs. For him there is no schism in the universe, no force opposed to God or capable of thwarting Him, no evil ineradicable by the soul, no limit set on human aspiration. Vice and disease he rebukes and pities. They are tainted, defective, miserable: yet not to be screamed at; rather to be cured and healed. He knows that purity is best, and health is best. But he also shows that what false modesty accounted unclean is the cleanest and the healthiest of all. In his return to nature he does not select inanimate nature, or single out the savage state. He takes man first, as the height and head of things; and after man the whole tract that human feet can traverse or human thought explore. Cities, arts, occupations, manufactures, have a larger place in his poetry than rivers or prairies; for these are nearer to man, more important to his destiny and education. He is the poet of fact, of the real, of what exists, of the last true, positive, and sole ontology.

After all, the great thing is, if possible, to induce people to study Whitman for themselves. I am convinced that, especially for young men, his spirit, if intelligently understood and sympathised with, must be productive of incalculable good. This, I venture to emphasise by relating what he did for me. I had received the ordinary English gentleman's education at Harrow and Oxford. Being physically below the average in health and strength, my development proceeded more upon the intellectual than the athletic side. In a word, I was decidedly academical, and in danger of becoming a prig. What was more, my constitution in the year 1865 seemed to have broken down, and no career in life lay open to me. In the autumn of that year, my friend Frederic Myers read me aloud a poem from "Leaves of Grass." We were together in his rooms at Trinity College, Cambridge and ; I can well remember the effect of his sonorous voice rolling out sentence after sentence, sending electric thrills through the very marrow of my mind.* I immediately procured the Boston edition of 1860-61, and began to study it attentively. It cannot be denied that much in Whitman puzzled and repelled me. But it was the æsthetic, not the moral, sensibility that suffered; for I felt at once that his method of treating sexual things (the common stumbling-block to beginners) was the right one, and wished that I had come across "Children of Adam" several years earlier. My academical prejudices, the literary instincts trained by two decades of Greek and Latin studies, the refinements of culture, and the exclusiveness of aristocratic breeding, revolted against the uncouthness, roughness, irregularity, coarseness, of the poet and his style. But, in course of a short time, Whitman delivered my soul of these debilities. As I have elsewhere said in print, he

* It was a piece from "Calamus," beginning "Long I thought that that knowledge alone would suffice me." Curiously enough, this has been omitted from subsequent editions, for what reasons I know not.

taught me to comprehend the harmony between the democratic spirit, science, and that larger religion to which the modern world is being led by the conception of human brotherhood, and by the spirituality inherent in any really scientific view of the universe. He gave body, concrete vitality, to the religious creed which I had been already forming for myself upon the study of Goethe, Greek and Roman Stoics, Giordano Bruno, and the founders of the evolutionary doctrine. He inspired me with faith, and made me feel that optimism was not unreasonable. This gave me great cheer in those evil years of enforced idleness and intellectual torpor which my health imposed upon me. Moreover, he helped to free me from many conceits and pettinesses to which academical culture is liable. He opened my eyes to the beauty, goodness and greatness which may be found in all worthy human beings, the humblest and the highest. He made me respect personality more than attainments or position in the world. Through him, I stripped my soul of social prejudices. Through him, I have been able to fraternise in comradeship with men of all classes and several races, irrespective of their caste, creed, occupation, and special training. To him I owe some of the best friends I now can claim —sons of the soil, hard workers, "natural and nonchalant," " powerful uneducated " persons.

Only those who have been condemned by imperfect health to take a back-seat in life so far as physical enjoyments are concerned, and who have also chosen the career of literary study, can understand what is meant by the deliverance from foibles besetting invalids and pedants for which I have to thank Walt Whitman.

What he has done for me, I feel he will do for others—for each and all of those who take counsel with him, and seek from him a solution of difficulties differing in kind according to the temper of the individual—if only they approach him in the right spirit of confidence and open-mindedness.